Get Ready, Set, Grow!

A Preplanned Calendar of Preschool Activities

by Eileen Morris and
Stephanie Pereau Crilly

Illustrated by Eileen Morris

Fearon Teacher Aids
a division of
David S. Lake Publishers
Belmont, California

W9-ACG-734

Special thanks to Eileen Morris for the many illustrations
contained in this book—*The Publisher*

Editorial director: Ina Tabibian
Editor: Robin E. Kelly
Designers: Terry McGrath and Emily Kissin
Cover designer: Emily Kissin
Design director: Eleanor Mennick
Production editor: Kimberly Pesavento
Manufacturing manager: Casimira S. Kostecki

ISBN-0-8224-5858-6

Library of Congress Catalog Card Number: 84–60318
Printed in the United States of America.

1. 9 8 7 6 5 4

THE PRESCHOOL TEACHER'S PLEDGE

Place your right hand over your left eye
and repeat after us:

Dear children,

I do solemnly promise to abide by these rules
or be struck down by a speeding tricycle.

I hereby promise to:

- try to be understanding and loving
  when things don't go right

- be encouraging and patient when
  you need my help

- give you lots of free and unstructured
  time to grow

- give you some structured times for
  learning and fun

- try to remember what it's like
  to be a kid

- enjoy you and love you a lot!

Contents

Introduction

Welcome to the world of preschoolers. These precious years from ages 3 through 5 are times of unlimited energy, exuberance, and curiosity. We have created this easy-to-use calendar for those of you working and playing with children during these joyous but challenging years. This calendar is packed full of lesson plans and ideas that will help your days run a little smoother and give your children lots of worthwhile learning activities. We hope that your days are filled with fun and that your preschoolers will be able to say, "Guess what I learned today!"

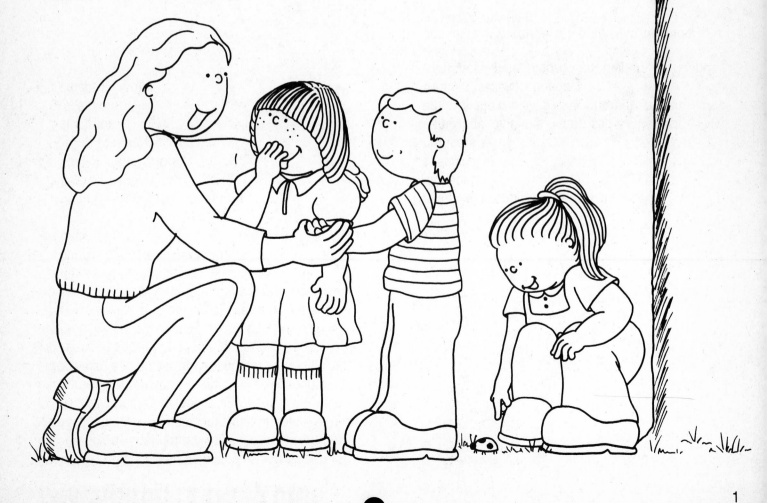

Description of Daily Unit

Each daily unit is a well-balanced lesson plan incorporating a variety of activities that focus on the weekly theme. These daily units can be followed step-by-step or modified to meet your needs. Your own background, interests, and abilities will generate enthusiasm and personalize each day. The time allotted for each activity and the amount of help needed by the children will depend on the children's ages, attention spans, and individual characteristics, as well as the number of children in your group. Read the daily unit before using it and be prepared. Throughout this book the following skills are used in the daily units:

listening (sound discrimination)
visual perception
visual discrimination
sorting/classifying
fine motor
gross motor
perceptual motor

The following subject areas are included:
alphabet
shapes
numbers 1–10
name, age, clothing, family, self-awareness
animals, life cycles, plants, nutrition, health
weather, seasons, holidays
awareness of neighborhoods, helpers, work and play places
concepts of warm/cold, big/small, over/under, beside, away, near

Definitions

The following terms are used to describe the segments of the daily units. The definitions explain the purpose of each segment and include suggestions for relevant activities.

Indoor Play

Indoor Play is a free play period at the beginning of each day. This activity gives the children a chance to adjust to their new environment. Before the children arrive, bring out a variety of toys from which they can choose. (See the list of suggested toys at right.) Occasionally we have listed an idea or game that can be added for variation.

Indoor Play gives children an excellent opportunity to develop language, social skills, motor control, and sensory awareness. Also, you can emphasize sharing and independence during this supervised yet unstructured time.

Suggested toys and play items:

Tinkertoys
blocks
crayons and paper
flannel board
magnetic letters and board
books
puppets
trucks
trains
planes
dishes
pots and pans
toy telephones
stuffed animals
playing cards
rice and measuring cups
Lincoln Logs
lock blocks
large boxes or cartons
dolls and doll clothes
blackboard and chalk
large stringing beads
dress-up clothes
mops and brooms
toy furniture and appliances
puzzles and games
catalogs

Children playing with very small or heavy objects require special supervision.

Art

The art ideas in this calendar reinforce the weekly theme. You can make the art projects more simple or more elaborate, depending on your children's abilities. While expanding the children's understanding of the theme, encourage creativity and self-expression. In lieu of the suggested project, you may want just to bring out paints, crayons, clay, or other art materials and give the children a chance to create their own projects. (Some ideas are given below.) Be sure to supervise the children at all times. As always, the watchword here is "safety."

Suggested art activities:

cutting or tearing paper shapes
pasting, gluing, or taping paper figures
shaping modeling clay or playdough
painting with watercolors and sponges, fingers, brushes, cotton-tipped swabs, or string
woodworking
stitching and sewing with blunt needles and loose-weave fabrics
making collages
creating sculptures

Here are some recipes to make homemade dough for modeling:

Playdough
3 c. flour
1½ c. salt
3 tbsp. oil
2 tbsp. cream of tartar
3 c. water
Mix and cook over very low heat until not sticky to touch.

Modeling Goop
2 c. salt
1 c. water
1 c. corn starch
Cook salt and ½ cup water for 4–5 minutes. Remove from heat. Add corn starch and ½ cup water. Return to heat. Stir until mixture thickens. Store goop in plastic bag.

Clay
4 c. flour
1 c. salt
1½ c. water
Mix ingredients.

Music

This segment provides a great opportunity for the children to gather around and direct some of their exuberance and nonstop energy into rhythmic discovery. Repetition is important when children are learning the words and tunes to songs. However, we have also included many nonrepetitious activities that will widen the children's understanding and allow them to explore movement and sound. For your convenience we have listed the words to the circle dances, songs, nursery rhymes, and finger plays in the back of this calendar.

Snack

Learning occurs during all phases of this activity, from preparation to cleanup. Children learn to measure and combine ingredients. They learn about hot and cold and about various stages of matter (solid, liquid, gas). Stirring, shaking, and spreading help develop coordination and motor control.

Allow the children to participate as much as they are capable, and snacktime will be a satisfying and rewarding experience for them. All they need from you is 1 cup of supervision, 2 handfuls of help when needed, and 10 tablespoons of patience and understanding mixed in.

When recipes require freezing or baking time, you may want to prepare the snack the day before or at the beginning of the day. Many recipes require heat sources (oven or stove). Be especially cautious so children do not get burned. Also, be aware of children's allergies. When a recipe or idea is not given or if necessary ingredients and resources are unavailable, select another snack idea from the index or create your own.

Learning Time

Learning Time is simply the lesson for the day. In some units, Learning Time is combined with the Snack segment. Each lesson is presented to expand the children's understanding of the weekly theme. We have incorporated many concepts that are important to the preschoolers' development and growing understanding of the world around them. All you need to do is to follow the step-by-step instructions with lots of enthusiasm and encouragement.

Outdoor Play

Outdoor Play is a supervised free-time period conducted outdoors or in a spacious indoor area. Listed below are some toys and play equipment that you might want to make available for the children. Allow them to choose. Occasionally we have included ideas or games for this activity that will add variety to your daily routine.

During this unstructured segment of the daily unit, situations will arise when you can encourage children's development of large muscle coordination, strength and balance, and social play.

Suggested toys and play equipment are:

balls
beanbags
balloons
bubble liquid and bubble-blowers
Frisbee
trucks
dolls
water toys and small pools or tubs of water
Hula Hoops
paintbrushes and buckets of water
riding toys
climbing equipment
sandbox with buckets and sand toys

Supervise outdoor play closely. Children playing games that involve throwing, climbing, or using sand water, or bubble liquid require special attention.

Storytime

This segment is a quiet, calm period for reading, telling stories, or sharing thoughts. Storytime will help stimulate the children's imaginations, listening and communication skills, and appreciation for books. Many stories mentioned are common fairy tales (most from the Grimms' collections). You can read or tell any version of these you wish. When the daily unit does not offer a Storytime suggestion, choose one of the following activities:

1. Select and read a book.
2. Tell a story.
3. Have a show-and-tell or sharing time.
4. Create a flannel board story. To make a flannel board, cover a heavy piece of cardboard or pressboard with flannel or felt. (A carpet sample also works well.) Make flannel board cutouts from coloring books. Or draw and cut out your own figures from paper or felt. Glue sandpaper on the back of the paper cutouts to make them adhere better to the flannel board.

Field Trip

A field trip is an outing that will increase the children's understanding of the weekly theme. Field trips require special planning. You should have the children's parents sign consent forms. And you may have to arrange for tours or at least get permission from the site managers to bring the group.

Transportation can be a problem sometimes. Occasionally, walking to the excursion site is appropriate. With adequate supervision, taking public transportation can add some adventure to the field trip. Check bus and train schedules and keep them available. Plan ahead for transporation needs.

Field trips will affect your daily unit schedule. For example, sometimes you will want to prepare the snack to bring along on the field trip. Often the field trip will provide information for other lessons.

Extended Day

We are well aware of the growing need for extended day-care, and we realize that many schools offer such programs. This calendar can be expanded to meet these needs by extending activities or adding new ones. All the segment activities have been alphabetized in the index at the back of this calendar to facilitate expansion of daily units.

January
Week 1

We're gonna build him inside so the sun won't melt him.

Winter

Indoor Play
See suggestions for unstructured play on page 3.

Art
Snowman

- scissors
- crayons
- white paper
- construction paper in assorted colors
- glue

Help the children:
(1) cut 3 circles of different sizes out of white paper;
(2) arrange them from smallest to largest and glue them onto construction paper;
(3) cut out and glue on (or color) additional features.

Music
Songs

Everyone can act out and sing "Melting Snowman" (tune of "I'm a Little Teapot").

    I'm a little snowman round and fat.
    Here is my broom, and here is my hat.
    When the sun comes out it's time to say,
    This is the end of me today!

"Twinkle, Twinkle"   "Pop! Goes the Weasel"

Circle Dances

"Ring around the Rosie"   "Hokey Pokey"

Snack/Learning Time
Snowball Shake

- milk
- vanilla ice cream
- shredded coconut

Help each child:
(1) fill a large cup ¾ full of milk;
(2) add 1 scoop ice cream;
(3) sprinkle coconut on top.

Outdoor Play
Children take turns pinning a nose on a snowman from the art lesson. Follow directions to Pin the Nose on the Pumpkin on page 83.

Storytime
Snowy Night

Have the children take turns completing a story that begins: "On a cold winter night I looked out the window and saw Mr. Snowman playing."

Indoor Play
See suggestions on page 3.

Art
Snow Sculpture

- **glue**
- **scissors**
- **construction paper**
- **paper plates**
- **marshmallows**

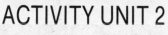

(1) Help each child glue marshmallows together on a paper plate to create a sculpture, an igloo, or a snowman.
(2) Have them cut other features out of construction paper and glue these features in place.

Music
Finger Plays and Songs
"Open, Shut Them"
"Two Little Blackbirds"
"I've Been Working on the Railroad"

Circle Dances
"Hokey Pokey"
"Looby Loo"

Snack
How about hot malted milk drinks?

Learning Time
Ice Melts

- **ice cubes**
- **paper towels and cups**

(1) Discuss hot and cold objects, such as ice, stoves, heaters, ice cream, snow, and fire.
(2) Let children observe the process of an ice cube melting. Ask children such questions as, Where does it go? How does it feel in your hand? In your mouth?
(3) Have them pretend to be ice cubes melting.

Outdoor Play
Ice Cube Drawing
If weather permits, let children use ice cubes to draw on cement outside.

Storytime
Read a story with descriptive passages. Have children close their eyes, imagine what the words describe, and verbally share the images they had.

Indoor Play
Use rice, measuring cups, and pitchers to develop pouring skills.

Art
Snowstorm

- **liquid starch or glue**
- **brush or cotton-tipped swabs**
- **construction paper**
- **rice**

Help the children:
(1) generously brush starch or glue onto paper;
(2) sprinkle rice on paper;
(3) shake off excess.

Music
Have the children wave scarves or streamers as they move to the rhythm of music.

Snack
Snowcone

- **crushed ice**
- **concentrated orange juice**
- **water**

Each child mixes 2 tbsp. juice with 2 tbsp. water and pours mixture over crushed ice.

Learning Time
What to Wear?
(1) Discuss temperature changes during different seasons.
(2) Discuss today's weather. ·
(3) Show assorted pieces of clothing one by one and ask, "Would you wear this today? Why?"

Outdoor Play
Mouse Trap
(1) One child is the CAT and turns away, with back toward others.
(2) The MICE (all others) sneak up behind the CAT and scratch (make noise).
(3) The CAT turns around and chases them back to their hole (some designated area).
(4) If the CAT tags a MOUSE before the MOUSE reaches the hole, the tagged child sits out until next game.
(5) Children take turns being the CAT.

Storytime
See page 7 for Storytime suggestions.

January
Week 2

What color are goldfish?

Colors

Indoor Play
See page 3.

Art
Traffic Lights

- pencils
- scissors
- green and red construction paper
- glue
- Popsicle sticks
- saucer

Help each child:
(1) trace 2 large circles on red paper and 2 on green, using saucer as pattern;
(2) cut out circles;
(3) glue red circles onto both sides of stick;
(4) repeat step 3 with green circles.

Music
Poem
Everyone can act out the "Color Poem."
  If you're wearing red, pat your head.
  If you're wearing blue, count to two.
  If you're wearing green, let your smile be seen.
  If you're wearing brown, hop up and down.
  If you're wearing yellow, jump like a funny fellow.
  If you're wearing black, pat your back.

Songs
"Happy and You Know It"   "Bingo"

Snack
Purple Finger Gelatin

- 12 oz. frozen grape juice (thawed)
- 3 pkgs. unflavored gelatin
- 1½ c. hot water

Children can help dissolve gelatin in water, stir in juice, and pour into oiled 9" × 13" pan. Chill. Cut into strips.

Learning Time
Red Light, Green Light
(1) Child chosen to be IT faces other children standing about 20 feet away. IT holds traffic lights from art lesson.
(2) When IT raises green traffic light, children walk forward. When IT changes to red light, they stop.
(3) Whoever touches IT first gets to be IT next.

Outdoor Play
See page 6.

Storytime
See page 7.

Indoor Play
See page 3.

Art
Crayon Tablecloth
- **tape**
- **shelf paper or butcher paper**
- **crayons**

(1) Cover table with paper. Tape paper down.
(2) The children can color large designs or pictures. Encourage full, sweeping arm movements.
(3) Use as a tablecloth during the snack.

Music
Put on records and have children move to music as if they are ballet dancers, rag dolls, or clowns.

Snack
Serve cereal and milk.

Learning Time
Jolly Ghost Story

(1) Cut same ghost shape out of construction paper in 6-8 colors, including white, red, and purple.
(2) Stack ghosts, placing white one on top.
(3) Hold ghosts up and begin story: "One day Jolly Ghost was hungry. He went to the refrigerator and ate some purple grapes. He looked in the mirror and saw he had turned purple. *(put white ghost in back of pile and show purple ghost)* He was so upset he ate a tomato, and to his surprise, he turned red." *(show red ghost)*
(4) Continue story, adding foods to match the ghost's color. End story by saying, "Finally he was so thirsty he drank some milk and turned white again."

Outdoor Play
Duck, Duck, Goose

(1) The group sits in a circle. Choose a child to be IT.
(2) IT walks around the outside of the circle, tapping each child on the shoulder and saying, "Duck."
(3) Then IT taps a child and says, "Goose."
(4) GOOSE stands up and chases IT around the circle, back to where the chase began.
(5) If IT gets back to the starting point without being tagged, IT takes GOOSE's spot in the circle and GOOSE becomes IT. If GOOSE tags IT, GOOSE returns to circle and IT continues to be IT.

Storytime
See page 7 for ideas.

Indoor Play
Sorting Buttons
Provide a variety of buttons. Supervise children as they:
(1) sort buttons into such different categories as size, color, shape, and number of holes;
(2) use buttons to create shapes on the floor.

Art
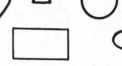
Color Shapes
- **scissors**
- **pencils**
- **tagboard**
- **construction paper in assorted colors**

(1) Out of tagboard cut various shapes to be used as patterns.
(2) Have children trace shapes on paper.
(3) Help children cut out shapes.

Music
Nursery Rhymes and Songs

"Jack and Jill"	"Little Miss Muffet"
"Humpty Dumpty"	"Bingo"

Circle Dances

"Hokey Pokey"	"Punchinello"

Snack
Hot apple cider is a great winter warm-up.

Learning Time
Color Hunt
- **color shapes from art lesson**
- **glue**
- **paper bags**

(1) Glue 1 color shape onto each bag.
(2) Hide the remaining color shapes.
(3) Let children find the hidden shapes, match them with the colors on the bags, and place them inside the bags.

Outdoor Play
Take Color Hunt game outdoors and let group play again.

Storytime
Colorful Story

(1) Give each child a different color shape from the art lesson.
(2) Tell a story, incorporating different colors into the plot.
(3) Children hold up the corresponding color shapes when colors are mentioned in the story.

January
Week 3

Are you the man who's gonna kick me out if I make too much noise?

In the City

Indoor Play
Bring out blocks for the group to build a city. Ask them to include walls, buildings, roads, and houses.

Art
City Buildings
- **paint**
- **construction paper**
- **cotton-tipped swabs**

Help children make outlines of buildings and roads by dipping swabs in paint and drawing on paper.

Music
Nursery Rhymes and Songs

"Hickory, Dickory Dock"   "Jack, Be Nimble"
"Jack and Jill"   "Baa, Baa, Black Sheep"
"Are You Sleeping?"   "Down by the Station"

Circle Dances

"Farmer in the Dell"   "Skip to My Lou"

Snack
How about trying bananas and sour cream?

Learning Time
Shadow Mime
(1) Direct a light source (a lamp or a slide projector) toward a wall. Turn it on.
(2) Stand between light and wall. Make shadows.
(3) Show children how to imitate people working in the city. For example, imitate a police officer directing traffic, a construction worker using a jack hammer, a bus driver, and a gas station attendant.
(4) Have the group guess the occupations imitated.
(5) Allow children to try shadow imitations.

Outdoor Play
Let children take chalk outdoors and draw designs on cement. Wash off designs with water.

Storytime
See page 7 for suggested activities.

Indoor Play
Let the children form roads with uncooked macaroni.

Art
City Mural

- **large piece of butcher paper or shelf paper**
- **magazines**
- **marking pens**
- **scissors**
- **glue**

(1) Draw roads and a few buildings on paper.
(2) Have children look in magazines for city scenes to cut out and glue onto the mural. Older children can draw their own city scene pictures on the mural.
(3) Display mural on wall.

Music
Finger Plays and Songs

"Two Little Blackbirds"   "Where Is Thumbkin?"
"Jack-in-the-Box"   "Twinkle, Twinkle"

Circle Dances

"Looby Loo"   "Hokey Pokey"
"Punchinello"

Snack/Learning Time
Glazed House Cookies

- **chilled cookie dough (basic sugar cookie recipe)**
- **egg whites**
- **water**
- **food coloring**
- **brushes**

(1) Roll out chilled dough.
(2) Help children cut out squares and triangles to form houses.
(3) Mix egg whites, water, and food coloring to the right consistency for spreading with a brush.
(4) Let children brush cookies with egg mixture.
(5) Bake cookies as directed in recipe.

Outdoor Play
Have appropriate supplies (such as shovels, rakes, brooms) available for outdoor cleanup.

Storytime
Tell stories using such position words as *inside*, *over*, *under*, *beside*, *above*, and *below*. For example: "I was above the cave, and the bear was inside."

Field Trip
A Visit to a City Spot
Consider the following excursion sites:

bakery	factory
airport	museum
library	bus terminal
construction site	car wash

Learning Time
City Rubbings
Bring lightweight paper and some crayons on city outing and have children:

(1) place paper on any flat, textured surface, such as a brick wall or a cement step;
(2) rub crayons back and forth across surface of paper;
(3) discuss different results.

Music
City Sounds

(1) Tape-record such city sounds as sirens, construction site noises, traffic, and voices in a crowd.
(2) Play back at a later time and have children identify sounds.
(3) Encourage children to listen for the "rhythm" of the city.

January
Week 4

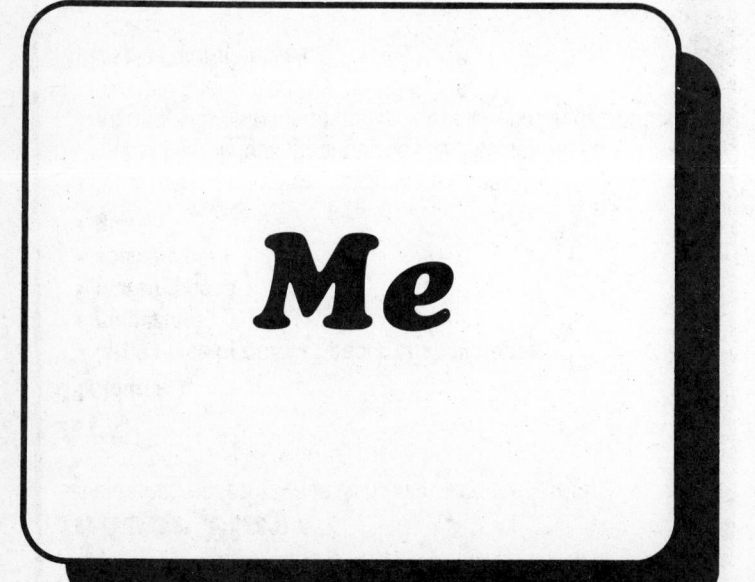

Indoor Play
Each child should look for reflections of himself or herself in mirrors, windows, and objects made of chrome and other shiny metals.

Art
My Own Clock
- **brass fasteners**
- **crayons**
- **arrows cut out of construction paper**
- **paper plates**

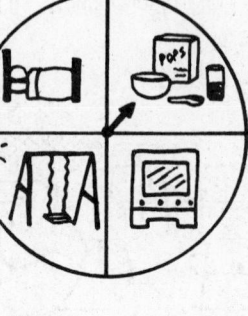

Help each child:
(1) divide plate into quarters;
(2) draw a daily activity in each quarter;
(3) attach arrow in center of plate with brass fastener.

Music
Songs
"I Am Special" (tune of "Are You Sleeping?")
  I am special, I am special.
  Look at me, you will see
  A very special person, a very special person.
  That is me, that is me.

Circle Dances
"Skip to My Lou"   "Ring around the Rosie"

Snack
Sample different kinds of crackers and cheeses.

Learning Time
What Do I Do Each Day?
(1) Use a clock from the art lesson and discuss daily activities in order of occurrence.
(2) Turn clock arrow to a daily activity and ask a child to act it out.
(3) Children can take turns acting out other daily activities, such as getting dressed, eating breakfast, going to play, and brushing teeth.

Outdoor Play
The children can look for shadows and do their own shadow dances.

Storytime
Read or tell the story of Aladdin and the lamp.

Indoor Play

Bring out scale and tape measure. Have children discover the height and weight of themselves and of each other.

Art

Things I Like

- **magazines or catalogs**
- **scissors**
- **paper plates**
- **marking pens**
- **glue**
- **string**

Help each child:

(1) print *Things I Like* on a plate;
(2) tear or cut out pictures of favorite things from magazines or catalogs;
(3) glue pictures onto paper plate;
(4) make a hole in top of plate and loop string through hole to hang up plate.

Music

Listening to Instruments

(1) Ask a child to select a rhythm instrument and play it while the others cover their eyes.
(2) Have the group guess the instrument played.
(3) The correct guesser takes the next turn.

Snack/Learning Time

Pizza Face

- **oregano**
- **catsup**
- **English muffins**
- **shredded cheese**
- **sliced olives**
- **chopped celery**
- **raisins**

The children can help prepare this snack.

(1) Spread catsup on muffins. Sprinkle on oregano.
(2) Make face on each muffin, using olives, celery, and raisins. Add cheese for hair.
(3) Place on cookie sheet and bake at 350° until cheese melts.

Outdoor Play

Children can take scarves or towels outdoors to use as capes. They can run with their capes, pretending to be the wind.

Storytime

Tell Me a Story

Let children take turns telling stories about themselves when they were younger.

Indoor Play

See page 3 for ideas.

Art

Face Puppets

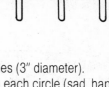

- **Popsicle sticks or straws**
- **construction paper**
- **scissors**
- **crayons**
- **stapler**

(1) Help each child cut out 3 circles (3″ diameter).
(2) Have the child draw a face on each circle (sad, happy, mean).
(3) Staple each circle on a stick or straw.

Music

Finger Plays and Songs

"Open, Shut Them"	"Five in the Bed"
"Are You Sleeping?"	"Itsy, Bitsy Spider"

Circle Dances

"Hokey Pokey"	"Punchinello"
"Ring around the Rosie"	"Skip to My Lou"

Snack

Apples and cheese go well together.

Learning Time

Making Faces

(1) Discuss various feelings—happiness, sadness, anger, meanness, surprise, fear.
(2) Demonstrate and have each child practice facial expressions while looking in a mirror.
(3) While children say poem below, have them hold up appropriate face puppet from art lesson. (Poem can be sung to "I'm a Little Teapot.")
Some little faces I have seen.
Some were sad, and some were mean.
But the one little face with a smile was best.
That was the happiest of all the rest.

Outdoor Play

Beanbag Toss

- **empty trash can**
- **sock**
- **1 c. beans**

(1) Let the children pour beans into sock.
(2) Knot open end and turn down cuff.
(3) Children can count tosses made into trash can.

Storytime

See page 7 for suggestions.

February
Week 1

How many numbers are in the alphabet?

Alphabet

Indoor Play
Use letters from Scrabble game to introduce alphabet. Capable children can practice spelling their names.

Art
Coloring Initials
- **crayons**
- **construction paper**

(1) Print each child's first initial in a very large block letter on paper.
(2) Child colors inside the letter.

Music
Songs
"Alphabet Song"
   A–B–C–D–E–F–G
   H–I–J–K–L–M–N–O–P
   Q–R–S–T–U–V
   W–X–Y and Z
   Now I know my A–B–C's.
   Next time won't you sing with me?
"This Old Man"   "Bingo"

Circle Dances
"Hokey Pokey"   "Looby Loo"
"Ring around the Rosie"

Snack/Learning Time
Winter Picnic
- **bag lunches or snacks**
- **sun cut out of yellow construction paper**
- **small toys**
- **tape**
- **towel or mat for each child**

(1) Select an appropriate area indoors to have a picnic.
(2) Place towels and toys on floor.
(3) Tape up sun to brighten a gloomy day.
(4) Enjoy a picnic and informal play with your group.

Outdoor Play
Recite the alphabet with the group. Bounce a ball among the group members and have everyone say the next letter each time the ball bounces.

Storytime
See page 7.

Indoor Play
Bring out alphabet blocks for free play.

Art
Pretzel Letters

- sea salt
- 1 loaf frozen bread dough (thawed)
- egg white mixed with 1 tsp. water

Help each child:
(1) pull off enough dough to form 1½″ ball;
(2) roll each ball into rope 12″ long;
(3) form rope into initial and let stand 20 minutes;
(4) brush with egg white and water mixture;
(5) sprinkle with salt and place on cookie sheet.
Bake at 350° until golden brown.

Music
Finger Plays and Songs

"Here Is the Beehive"   "Happy and You Know It"
"Teasing Mr. Crocodile"   "Bingo"
"Five in the Bed"   "I'm a Little Teapot"

Circle Dances

"London Bridge"   "Farmer in the Dell"

Snack
Children can eat their pretzel letters from the art lesson.

Learning Time
Tracing Letters
(1) Darken room.
(2) Use flashlight to "draw" letters on wall. Ask children to guess the letters.
(3) Let children take turns drawing flashlight letters.
(4) Turn lights on. Let children trace letters on each other's backs with fingers. Each child tries to guess the letter drawn on his or her back.

Outdoor Play
Children can ride bikes or wagons along chalk-drawn roads.

Storytime
Beginning Sounds
Tell a story. Give beginning sound clues for some missing words and ask the group to provide the full words. For example: "The farmer was milking the c_____ . I heard a p_____ say, 'Oink, oink.' "

Indoor Play
See page 3.

Art
Matching Letters

- paper plates
- marking pens
- brass fasteners
- 2 arrows cut out of construction paper

(1) Divide plate into 8–16 sections.
(2) Print a letter in each section, using each letter twice. Use all capitals or all small letters; don't mix them.
(3) Using fasteners, attach 2 arrows to center of plate.
(4) Have children point arrows to matching letters.

Music
Nursery Rhymes and Songs

"Mary Had a Little Lamb"   "Itsy, Bitsy Spider"
"Row Your Boat"   "Down by the Station"

Records
Have children listen to records and take turns pantomiming singers.

Snack
Alphabet soup makes letters fun.

Learning Time
Labels in the House

- index cards
- masking tape
- pens

(1) Have children tell you the beginning sounds of the words for objects in the room.
(2) Print the letter or letters of each beginning sound on an index card.
(3) Tape each card to the appropriate object in the room, such as D on door.

Outdoor Play
Sorting Buttons

- egg carton
- buttons in different colors or uncooked pasta in different shapes
- plastic container

(1) Place all objects in plastic container.
(2) Supervise children as they sort items by color or shape into separate compartments of egg carton.

Storytime
Read or tell the story of Snow White.

February
Week 2

Look what I made for you! HAPPY VALENTINE'S DAY!

Valentine Fun

Indoor Play
See page 3.

Art
Magic Valentines from Crayon Rubbings

- crayons
- paper clips
- 2 sheets of white paper for each child
- paper hearts (all sizes)

Help each child:
(1) put hearts on 1 sheet of paper and place other sheet on top;
(2) clip pages together to keep them from slipping;
(3) rub the side of crayon over surface of paper. Hearts will appear "like magic."

Music
Finger Plays and Songs

"Five Little Monkeys"	"Are You Sleeping?"
"Open, Shut Them"	"Row Your Boat"
"Five in the Bed"	"Happy and You Know It"

Circle Dances

"Farmer and the Dell"	"Ring around the Rosie"

Snack
Use your imagination!

Learning Time
Heart Puzzles

- scissors
- marking pens
- hearts from art lesson

(1) Cut hearts in half, leaving a zigzag edge.
(2) Number both sides of heart with same number.
(3) Let children mix and match heart halves.

Outdoor Play
Heart, Heart, Who's Got the Heart?
Using a small red heart or button, children can play by the rules to Who's Got the Button on page 78.

Storytime
Let the group share reasons why we say "I love you" to special people.

Indoor Play

See page 3.

Art

Laced Heart

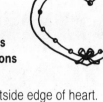

- hole punch
- cardboard heart shapes
- long shoelaces or ribbons with ends taped

(1) Punch holes around outside edge of heart.
(2) Let children weave shoelace or ribbon through holes.
(3) Help children tie ends in a bow.

Music

Patting to the Music

(1) Play records with easy-to-follow beats.
(2) Select a child to lead the group. Leader pats parts of body to the music. Others follow the leader.
(3) Children should take turns being leader.

Snack

Sweethearts

- refrigerator biscuits
- sugar and cinnamon mixture
- melted butter

Let children:
(1) separate biscuits and mold each into a heart shape;
(2) roll it in butter, then in sugar and cinnamon mixture.
Bake according to directions on package.

Learning Time

Valentine Stick

- valentine cards (store-bought)
- glue
- Popsicle stick

Each child can:
(1) select a valentine and attach it to a stick;
(2) sit behind a sofa, chair, or table to use as stage;
(3) create a story or perform nursery rhymes.

Outdoor Play

Let children count how many times they can catch a beanbag or a ball.

Storytime

See page 7.

Indoor Play

Let children stack blocks.

Art

Valentine Collage

- glue
- scissors
- magazines
- large, red construction paper hearts

Children can:
(1) cut or tear favorite pictures from a magazine;
(2) glue magazine pictures on heart shape.

Music

Nursery Rhymes and Songs

"Little Miss Muffet"	"Yankee Doodle"
"Humpty Dumpty"	"I'm a Little Teapot"
"Hickory, Dickory Dock"	"Pop! Goes the Weasel"

Circle Dances

"Looby Loo"	"Mulberry Bush"

Snack

Children can munch on red apples.

Learning Time

Post Office Valentine

- small paper bags
- valentine cards (store-bought)
- crayons

(1) Give each child a bag and some valentines. Have child decorate the bag.
(2) Children can take turns being a mail carrier who delivers valentines. Use bags as mailboxes.

Outdoor Play

Let children talk chalk outdoors and draw valentines on the cement. The chalk washes off with water.

Storytime

As you tell the story of Little Red Riding Hood, have the children act out the words.

February
Week 3

Presidents' Birthdays

Field Trip

A Visit to the Library or a Museum
(1) Look with the children for a patriotic display.
(2) Help group look for books on Lincoln or Washington.
(3) Find out in advance whether there is a story hour.

Snack/Learning Time

Patriotic Bon Bons

- ¼ tsp. vanilla
- 3 oz. cream cheese
- 2½ c. powdered sugar
- dash of salt
- coconut
- red and blue food coloring

Help children prepare this snack. You may want to do step 5 by yourself.
(1) Beat cream cheese and sugar until smooth.
(2) Beat in vanilla and salt.
(3) Form small balls with mixture.
(4) Separate coconut in 3 bowls.
(5) Leave first bowl of coconut white. Color second one red and third one blue.
(6) Roll balls in different color coconut.
(7) Refrigerate snack before serving.

Outdoor Play

Froggy, Froggy
(1) All children form a circle and squat down.
(2) Choose a child to be IT. Others are FROGS.
(3) IT hops over to any FROG and asks, "Froggy, Froggy, who's your neighbor?" That FROG responds, "I don't know, but I'll go see."
(4) IT takes FROG's place in circle, and FROG becomes IT.
(5) The new IT hops over to another FROG, and the game begins again.

Indoor Play
Bring out Lincoln Logs for free play.

Art
Washington's Hat

- **scissors**
- **stapler**
- **construction paper**

(1) For each child, cut out a shape (approximately 2″ × 7″), using the pattern shown.

(2) The children use their shapes to outline and cut 2 more identical shapes.

(3) Staple ends of 3 shapes together to form triangular hat for each child.

Music
Washington's March

- **masking tape**
- **drum, or spoon and pan**
- **Washington's hats from art lesson**

(1) Tape large circle on floor.

(2) Children wear their hats and march around circle to the beat of a drum.

(3) Change pace from fast to slow. Have children try skipping, walking, and running.

Snack
Try some cherry pie with milk.

Learning Time
Being a Leader

(1) Discuss the job of a president and what it means to be a leader.

(2) Let children take turns being the leader and having the others follow.

Outdoor Play
When dressing for outdoors, have the children try to dress themselves. They can attempt snapping, buckling, lacing, tying, zipping, and buttoning.

Storytime
Read a story. Have children retell the story.

Indoor Play
See suggestions on page 3.

Art
Lincoln's Log Cabin

(1) For younger children, sketch a simple cabin design. Older children can design their own cabins.

(2) Help children glue pretzel sticks onto paper to make log cabins.

Music
Roll Ball to Music

(1) Have children sit in a circle. Play records.

(2) Children roll a ball to each other.

(3) When the music stops, the one who has the ball is "caught."

(4) Continue playing until only 1 player is left.

Songs

"Yankee Doodle" "Happy and You Know It"
"Pop! Goes the Weasel" "Twinkle, Twinkle"

Snack/Learning Time
Applesauce

- **water**
- **6 apples**
- **1 tbsp. cinnamon**

(1) Peel and quarter apples. Remove cores.

(2) Cook apples in water until soft. Cool.

(3) Let the children mash the apples and add the cinnamon.

Outdoor Play
See page 6 for activity suggestions.

Storytime
Long Ago

(1) Read from a book that has stories about Washington and/or Lincoln.

(2) Discuss how times have changed since Washington or Lincoln lived. For example, talk about what it was like before we had electricity, cars, airplanes, or certain modern conveniences.

February

Week 4

I'm three fingers old today!

Numbers

Indoor Play
See page 3.

Art
Numbered Fish
- **marking pen**
- **fish pattern**
- **construction paper**
- **paper clips**
- **scissors**

Help children:
(1) use the pattern to outline several fish and then cut them out;
(2) write a different number between 1 and 10 on each fish;
(3) attach a paper clip to nose of each fish.

Music
Finger Plays

"Here Is the Beehive" "Wheels on the Bus"
"Teasing Mr. Crocodile" "Ten Little Indians"

Circle Dances

"Mulberry Bush" "Looby Loo"
"Punchinello" "Ring around the Rosie"

Snack
Serve bananas in jello.

Learning Time
Fishing for Numbers

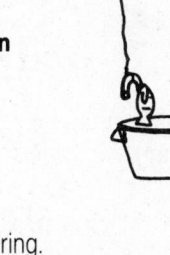

- **numbered fish from art lesson**
- **magnet**
- **pole (dowel)**
- **string**
- **bucket or tub**

(1) Tie string to pole.
(2) Tie magnet on loose end of string.
(3) Place numbered fish in the bucket.
(4) Let children take turns fishing. They hang the magnet at the end of the fishing line into the tub, and the magnet will attract the paper clip on a fish.
(5) The children should say the number on each fish they catch.

Outdoor Play
In sandbox, children can draw numbers with finger or stick. Words for "The Number Song" are on pages 68 and 69.

Storytime
See page 7.

Indoor Play

Taking Inventory

Give children paper and crayons and help them take inventory of items in the play area.

Art

Candles on a Cake

- playdough (recipe on page 4)
- small candles
- plastic lids

Let each child:
(1) make a pretend birthday cake out of playdough;
(2) use plastic lid as plate to display cake;
(3) place candles in cake and count candles.

Music

Nursery Rhymes and Songs

"Hickory, Dickory Dock"   "Down by the Station"
"Jack, Be Nimble"   "Row Your Boat"

Circle Dances

"London Bridge"   "Ring around the Rosie"

Snack

See page 5.

Learning Time

Five Little Monkeys

- flannel board or carpet sample
- construction paper
- tape
- scissors

(1) Cut 5 monkey shapes and 1 bed shape out of construction paper.
(2) Tape bed to flannel board. Tape monkeys over bed.
(3) Lead the group in singing "Five Little Monkeys" (words on page 103). Let a child remove a monkey from the board after each verse.
(4) Children can take turns removing monkeys.

Outdoor Play

Walnut Toss

Children try tossing whole walnuts into an empty coffee can from various distances and then count the number they get in the can.

Storytime

Tell a story about a child whose names begins with a *B* (or any letter). Continue story about the child eating, going places, and doing things. Use words that begin with *B* (or the featured letter).

Indoor Play

Playing Cards

Remove face cards from a deck of playing cards and have children put numbers in sequence, play "fish," throw cards into a hat, and match similar cards.

Art

Cutting Practice

- plastic bags
- scissors
- paper

Have children cut different shapes, small pieces, or fringed edges. They can save their cuttings in bags.

Music

Relaxing to Music

(1) Play relaxing records and have children lie down.
(2) Have children tighten then relax specific parts of body, such as leg, arm, fist, jaw, toes.

Snack/Learning Time

Count-a-Snack

- 5 kinds of snacks, such as raisins, popcorn, crackers, pretzels, Cheerios
- 5 index cards
- pen
- paper plates

(1) Write a different number between 1 and 10 on each index card.
(2) Fold each card and prop up next to a plate.
(3) Put a different snack on each plate.
(4) Give each child an empty paper plate.
(5) Have children take from each plate the number of pieces indicated on index card.

Outdoor Play

Lily Pad Jump

(1) Place 5-10 carpet samples on the ground to represent lily pads.
(2) Children can jump like frogs from lily pad to lily pad, counting each jump.

Storytime

See page 7.

March

Week 1

Did you see which way my bug collection went?

Science

Indoor Play
See page 3.

Art
Object Pictures
- paper
- crayons
- paste
- assorted items, such as Band-Aids, bows, straws, Popsicle sticks

Let each child:
(1) paste 1 item on paper;
(2) draw an appropriate picture around the item.

Music
Finger Plays and Songs

"Wheels on the Bus" "Two Little Blackbirds"
"This Old Man" "I'm a Little Teapot"

Circle Dances

"Ring around the Rosie" "Skip to My Lou"

Snack
Popsicle Freeze
- fruit juice
- paper cups
- Popsicle sticks
- fruit, such as cherries, strawberries, or pineapple

Help children:
(1) blend fruit juice and fruit;
(2) pour juice into cups, insert sticks, and freeze.

Learning Time
What Melts?
(1) Place an ice cube on a plate and have children watch it melt.
(2) Light a candle. Supervise carefully while children watch wax melt and drip.
(3) Show other solids that will melt easily and become liquids: crayons, chocolate, gelatin.

Outdoor Play
Magnifying Glass
(1) Give children paper bags and have them collect living and nonliving things, such as insects, bark, sugar, fabric, and stones.
(2) Provide a few magnifying glasses through which children can examine their collected objects.

Storytime
Object Stories
Begin telling a story based on one of the object pictures from the art lesson. Let the children take turns finishing your story or telling their own.

Indoor Play
Yes/No Magnets

- **2 boxes (one marked *yes*, one *no*)**
- **magnet**
- **assorted items, such as rubber bands, paper, buttons, nails, crayons, paper clips, plastic, coins**

Let the children discover which items the magnet will pick up and which ones it won't pick up. They can place each item in the appropriate box.

Art
Rock Mosaic

- **pencil**
- **pebbles**
- **glue**
- **heavyweight paper**

Have each child:
(1) draw a design on paper;
(2) fill in areas of the drawing by gluing on pebbles.

Music
Play symphonic music and let children do interpretive dances.

Snack
Vegetable Dip

- **1 cube beef or vegetable bouillon**
- **hot water**
- **3 oz. cream cheese**
- **1 tsp. grated Parmesan cheese**
- **⅛ tsp. garlic powder**
- **raw vegetables**

Children can help:
(1) dissolve bouillon in 3 tsp. hot water;
(2) beat in cream cheese and other ingredients.
Use as a dip for assorted raw vegetables.

Learning Time
Rock Collections

- **rocks**
- **water**
- **hammer**
- **egg cartons**

(1) Break rocks with hammer.
(2) Have the children place rocks in water to bring out colors.
(3) Then they can sort rocks in the egg cartons.

Outdoor Play
Let the group take magnets in the sandbox and discover what happens with the sand.

Storytime
See page 7.

Indoor Play
The children can stir sugar or salt into water and observe the physical change as it dissolves.

Art
Crystal Garden

- **pieces of brick, soft coal, or coke**
- **dish**
- **4 tbsp. water**
- **4 tbsp. liquid bluing**
- **4 tbsp. iodized salt**
- **1 tbsp. ammonia**
- **food coloring**

(1) Place pieces of brick in dish.
(2) Mix last 5 ingredients together and pour into dish.
(3) In a few hours the garden will take on interesting shapes for the children to see.

Music
Finger Plays and Songs

"Here Is the Beehive"   "Jack-in-the-Box"
"Five Little Monkeys"   "Teddy Bear"

Snack
Making Butter

- **heavy whipping cream**
- **jar with lid**
- **crackers**

(1) Fill jar half full of cream and put on lid.
(2) The children can take turns shaking jar rapidly until liquid separates.
(3) Then they can spread the butter on crackers.

Learning Time
Chemical Reaction

- **vinegar**
- **baking soda**
- **a glass**

In a glass, mix vinegar and soda together. The group can observe the fizzy chemical reaction.

Outdoor Play
Electricity Outdoors
Blow up and knot balloons. Children can rub balloons against rug or wool clothes and stick balloons to their hair or the wall. They may also enjoy playing balloon volleyball.

Storytime
See page 7.

March
Week 2

C'mon...
Hold still...
We half'ta
be green
today.

Saint Patrick's Day and More

Indoor Play
See page 3.

Art
Green Hats
- green paint (liquid type)
- 16" x 20" sheets of newspaper
- sponge (cut into 1" x 2" pieces)
- plastic lids

Help each child:
(1) fold paper in half, short end to short end;
(2) fold the top corners over to the center;
(3) fold up the top layer of lower portion, as shown;
(4) turn hat over and fold up bottom layer to match other side;
(5) place small amount of paint in lid, press sponge in paint, and stamp design on hat.

Music
St. Patrick's Parade
- coffee cans with lids
- green hats from art lesson

Children can make drums out of coffee cans with lids. Wearing their hats, children beat drums and march to the rhythm.

Snack
Try some limeade to reinforce the color green.

Learning Time
Hiding the Shamrock
(1) Cut a shamrock out of construction paper.
(2) Choose a child to be IT.
(3) While others cover their eyes, IT hides the shamrock within a designated area.
(4) All players open their eyes and try to find the shamrock. The finder gets to be IT next.

Outdoor Play
Use sticks, twigs, leaves, or rocks to create outdoor trails for the group to follow.

Storytime
Read from a collection of Irish fairy tales.

Indoor Play
See page 3.

Art
Green House

- **construction paper**
- **crayons**
- **scissors**
- **glue**
- **magazines with color illustrations and photos**

Each child can:
(1) draw a big house on paper and cut it out;
(2) find pictures of green items in magazines and tear or cut them out;
(3) glue pictures on the house.

Music
Nursery Rhymes and Songs

"Jack and Jill"   "Row Your Boat"
"Humpty Dumpty"   "Down by the Station"
"Are You Sleeping?"   "Baa, Baa, Black Sheep"

Circle Dances

"Punchinello"   "Ring around the Rosie"

Snack/Learning Time
Salad

- **lettuce**
- **carrots**
- **celery**
- **tomatoes**
- **radishes**
- **salad dressing**

(1) Children can tear lettuce and place in bowls.
(2) Cut up other vegetables and add to salads.
(3) Let children pour dressing on their salads.

Outdoor Play
Hot Potato

- **ball, beanbag, or potato**
- **whistle**

(1) Children sit in a circle and pass an object to each other as fast as possible, acting as if the object is hot.
(2) The player caught holding the object when you whistle is out until the next game. Those who are out can watch the game continue until only 1 player is left.

Storytime
Each child tells a story describing 3 wishes.

Field Trip
Visit to Duck Pond or Playground

(1) Take stale bread so children can feed the ducks or birds.
(2) Be sure to pack a snack. How about some hard-boiled eggs and carrot sticks?

Art
Over the Rainbow

- **crayons or paint**
- **large paper**

(1) Draw a huge rainbow for the group to color.
(2) Have the children fill in the arches with different colors.

Learning Time
Placing Beanbags

(1) Make beanbags by following directions on page 15.
(2) Ask group to follow your instructions, using the beanbags.
(3) Give directions that use such words as *above*, *behind*, *between*, *beside*, and *below*. For example:
Place the beanbag on your foot.
Place the beanbag between your knees.
Place the beanbag under your chin.
Place the beanbag above your head.
(4) Let the children make up their own beanbag directions.

March

Week 3

Will you please teach my kite how to fly?

Spring

Indoor Play
Bring out scissors and old catalogs, books, or magazines for cutting practice.

Learning Time
Spring Walk
(1) Discuss signs of spring with the group.
(2) Take a walk together. Encourage everyone to look for birds, bugs, blossoms, buds, and other signs of spring.
(3) They can collect in paper bags the "treasures" found along the way. Confine treasures to stones, twigs, and fallen items.

Music
Finger Plays and Songs

"Open, Shut Them"	"I'm a Little Teapot"
"Wheels on the Bus"	"Down by the Station"

Circle Dances

"Hokey Pokey"	"Farmer in the Dell"
"Punchinello"	"Ring around the Rosie"

Records
Lead the group in different movements to music. Gallop, skate, skip, run, tiptoe, and hop to the beat.

Snack
Nachos

- **corn chips**
- **cheese**

Melt cheese and pour it over corn chips. Cool slightly.

Art
Spring Collage

- **paper plates**
- **crayons or marking pens**
- **glue**
- **paper bags with treasures from spring walk**

(1) Help each child print *Spring* on plate.
(2) Child can then glue treasures onto plate.

Outdoor Play
Have children sit quietly in a circle and count how many different sounds they hear. Ask them to listen for birds chirping, airplanes flying by, and wind blowing.

Storytime
Have group act out the story "Snow White and the Seven Dwarfs."

Indoor Play
Golf

- plastic balls
- wooden spoons
- tin can

Lay tin can on side. Show children how to use a wooden spoon to gently hit ball into can. Then let them "golf."

Art
Blossoming Tree

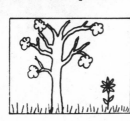

- popped popcorn
- construction paper
- marking pens or crayons
- glue

Help each child:
(1) draw a tree trunk and branches;
(2) glue popcorn on branches for blossoms;
(3) color additional features.

Music
"Spring Song" (tune of "Are You Sleeping?")
  I see robins, I see birds' nests,
  Butterflies too, flowers too.
  Everything is growing.
  The wind is gently blowing.
  Spring is here, spring is here!

Snack
Make extra popcorn during the art lesson for the snack.

Learning Time
(1) Discuss signs of spring: warmer weather, days growing longer, spring flowers.
(2) Show pictures of buds. Explain how trees get new leaves and blossoms.
(3) Tell children that spring is the time of year when bears come out of hibernation, birds begin to nest, and farmers plant crops.

Outdoor Play
See page 6.

Storytime
Create a story with a problem. For example, tell about a little girl who wants a puppy but has no place to keep it. Let the children take turns giving a solution to the problem.

Indoor Play
See page 3.

Art
Pussy Willows

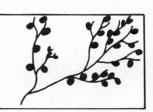

- glue
- cotton balls
- construction paper
- brown paint
- straws

(1) Put a few drops of paint in center of paper.
(2) Children blow through straws to spread paint.
(3) After paint dries, they can glue cotton balls on paper for blossoms.

Music
Nursery Rhymes and Songs

"Hickory, Dickory Dock"	"Mary Had a Little Lamb"
"Jack and Jill"	"Happy and You Know It"
"Jack, Be Nimble"	"Teddy Bear"

Circle Dances

"London Bridge"	"Ring around the Rosie"

Snack/Learning Time
Spring Picnic

(1) Spread a blanket on the ground and set out such picnic items as a thermos, napkins, paper plates and cups, utensils, cooler.
(2) Choose a child to be a mischievous little squirrel who takes 1 item while the others cover their eyes.
(3) Children then try to guess which item is missing.
(4) Enjoy some picnic food after the game.

Outdoor Play
Clothespins in the Bucket

- clothespins
- plastic bucket

Children take turns standing over bucket, trying to drop in clothespins and counting how many they get in.

Storytime
See page 7.

March

Week 4

Music

Indoor Play

Bring out play telephones and have the group practice dialing telephone numbers.

Art

Drawing to Music

- **crayons**
- **records and record player**
- **large pieces of newsprint**

(1) Spread out papers and give each child a crayon.
(2) Play a record and have children draw to the rhythm.
(3) Change records. Have children exchange crayons and draw to the new rhythm.
(4) After several records, point out design changes due to rhythm change.

Music

Musical Chairs

(1) Line up chairs (1 less than the number of players).
(2) Children walk around chairs while music plays and sit down when you stop the music.
(3) The child left standing leaves the game. Remove a chair. Game continues until only 1 player remains. Game begins again.

Snack

Let the children pour milk over crispy rice cereal and listen for sound.

Learning Time

Low and High Sounds

- **a glass**
- **water**
- **metal spoon**

(1) Tap empty glass with spoon. Have children listen carefully to the sound. Children can sing "Jingle Bells" while taking turns tapping the rhythm on the glass.
(2) Pour in small amount of water. Tap glass and have children listen again. Ask, "What happened to the sound? Is it higher or lower?"
(3) Repeat step 2, adding more water.
(4) Children can sing again while tapping the rhythm on the glass. *Make sure they tap lightly!*

Outdoor Play

See page 6.

Storytime

See page 7.

Indoor Play

See page 3.

Art

Maracas

- 2 paper cups
  for each child
- marking pens
- tape
- beans or rice
- crepe paper streamers

Help children:

(1) place beans or rice in 1 cup;
(2) tape the other cup upside down on top of first cup;
(3) decorate cups with marking pens;
(4) tape crepe paper streamers to cup ends.

Music

Crossing the River

(1) On the floor, make lines with chalk or tape to represent banks of a river. River should be several feet wide.
(2) Have children line up along one bank. Play music or clap your hands while children continually cross the river.
(3) When music stops, the children caught in the river must "dry out" (sit out) for one turn. Then they reenter the game.

Snack/Learning Time

Popcorn Dance

- popcorn (and oil, if needed)
- popcorn popper

(1) Pop popcorn. Have children observe, smell, and listen to it pop.
(2) The group can pretend to be popcorn popping while they sing "I'm a Little Corn Kernel" (tune of "I'm a Little Teapot").

    I'm a little corn kernel in a cup.
    Put me in a pot and heat me up.
    Listen to the popping sound I make.
    Pop, pop, pop is what I say.

Outdoor Play

Children can take their maracas from art lesson outside for musical outdoor play.

Storytime

Have children turn pages as your read a story.

Indoor Play

See page 3.

Art

Tambourines

- beans
- paper plates
- tape
- crayons or marking pens

Help each child:

(1) place a few beans on a plate;
(2) cover it with another plate turned upside down;
(3) tape plates together;
(4) decorate tambourine with crayons or pens.

Music

Tambourine Play

The children can shake and tap their tambourines from art lesson to these songs:

"Twinkle, Twinkle"	"Teddy Bear"
"Pop! Goes the Weasel"	"Yankee Doodle"

Circle Dances

"Punchinello"	"Looby Loo"

Snack

Pudding Sandwich

- instant pudding and milk
- graham crackers

(1) Children can help make pudding.
(2) Then they can spread pudding between crackers.
(3) Sandwiches can be frozen or eaten right away.

Learning Time

Musical Glasses

(1) Put 3 glasses in a row and pour just enough water in each glass to make the notes in the first line of "Are You Sleeping?" (do, re, mi, do).
(2) Choose 3 children to "play" the glasses with metal spoons while everyone sings "Are You Sleeping?" Change players.
(3) Let the group experiment with other tunes.

Outdoor Play

Pudding Finger Play

- pudding (leftovers from snack)
- aprons
- plastic place mats

Children can place pudding on mats and experiment.

Storytime

See page 7.

April
Week 1

Easter and Passover

Indoor Play
Make a batch of playdough (recipe on page 4) and let children form eggs and baskets.

Art
Dyeing Eggs

- hard-boiled eggs
- crayons
- water
- empty egg carton
- masking tape
- aprons
- cups or plastic containers
- food coloring or egg-dyeing kits

(1) Prepare dye and place in cups or containers.
(2) Have children gently draw on eggs with crayons or tear small pieces of tape and place on eggs.
(3) After children put on aprons, they can gently place eggs in dye.
(4) Remove eggs from dye and dry them in egg carton.

Music
Everyone can act out "The Egg Dyeing Song" (tune of "Mulberry Bush").

> This is the way we dye our eggs,
> Dye our eggs, dye our eggs.
> This is the way we dye our eggs
> So early Easter morning.

Other verses:
> This is the way we hide our eggs . . .
> This is the way we eat our eggs . . .

Snack
Children can eat hard-boiled eggs from art lesson.

Learning Time
Plastic Egg Games

- 12 colorful plastic eggs
- masking tape
- marking pen
- dried beans

(1) Game 1, Numbered Eggs: Using tape and pen, label each plastic egg with a number. Have child place appropriate number of beans in each egg.
(2) Game 2, Color Match Eggs: Children take apart all eggs and rematch the colored halves.
(3) Game 3, Egg Toss: In pairs, children toss egg back and forth, moving back 1 step after each successful toss. They must begin again when they drop the egg.

Outdoor Play
Have an Easter egg hunt outdoors, using plastic eggs.

Storytime
See page 7.

Indoor Play

How about an indoor egg hunt with eggs cut from paper?

Art

Hiding Bunnies

- white construction paper
- green paint
  or green crayons
- cotton balls
- glue

Each child will:

(1) paint or draw grass all over paper;
(2) glue cotton balls on paper to represent bunnies;
(3) take turns counting aloud the hiding bunnies.

Music

Everyone can sing and act out "Easter Hop" (tune of "Farmer in the Dell").

  Now point your left toe out.
  Then point your right toe out.
  Take a hop *(hop forward)*
  And take a hop. *(hop backward)*
  That's what this game's about.
Other verses:
  Now place your left heel out . . .
  Now put your left hand out . . .

Snack/Learning Time

Funny Bunny Salad

- pear halves
- raisins
- almonds
- maraschino cherries
- marshmallows

Each child can:

(1) place pear half on a plate with cut side facing down;
(2) use marshmallow for tail, cherry half for mouth, raisins for eyes, and almonds for ears.

Outdoor Play

See page 6.

Storytime

Use bunny pictures from art lesson. Have each child tell why his or her bunnies are hiding.

Indoor Play

Make playdough (recipe on page 4) and have children shape foods that resemble Passover feast.

Art

Matzo Cover

- ribbon or shoelace
- hole punch
- crayons
- 9" x 12" sheets of construction paper

(1) Fold each paper in half.
(2) Punch holes around folded edge and 2 other edges.
(3) Help each child weave ribbon or shoelace through holes, tie ends, and decorate cover with crayons.

Music

Everyone can sing "Passover Song" (tune of "Row Your Boat") before looking for a hidden matzo.

  Hide, hide, hide the matzo.
  Let's play hide and seek.
  Close your eyes and count to ten.
  And then we get to peek. *(yell, "Find the matzo!")*

Snack/Learning Time

Charoses (Fruit Salad)

- ½ lemon rind (grated)
- 1 c. chopped apple
- ¼ c. chopped walnuts
- 1 tsp. honey
- ½ tsp. cinnamon
- 1 tbsp. grape juice

The group can mix ingredients.

Outdoor Play

Hot or Cold Matzo

- matzo or cracker
- matzo cover from art lesson

(1) Place the matzo in the cover and choose a child to be IT. IT hides the covered matzo, and other children try to find the matzo.
(2) IT says "hot" if children are getting near and "cold" if they're moving away from matzo.
(3) The first child to find matzo becomes IT.

Storytime

A Walk to Grandma's

Everyone sits in a circle. Making hand motions that children repeat after you, tell story: "Let's go for a walk to Grandma's. *(pat legs)* There's some bushes. *(point)* Let's go through them. *(make an opening motion)* Back on the walk *(pat legs)* and what do I see?" Continue story, using action words.

April
Week 2

It's easy! Just think chocolate!

Farm Animals

Indoor Play

Children can use blocks to build corrals and fences for toy farm animals.

Art

Animal Puppet

- **paper lunch bags**
- **construction paper or small felt pieces**
- **glue**

(1) Have each child glue paper or felt pieces on bottom of bag to create an animal face.
(2) With hand inside bag, child manipulates animal's mouth by opening and closing hand.

Music

Finger Plays and Songs

"Two Little Blackbirds"   "Old MacDonald's Farm"

"Teasing Mr. Crocodile"   "Five Little Monkeys"

Circle Dances

"Hokey Pokey"   "Farmer in the Dell"

Snack

Peachy Chick

- **peach halves**
- **maraschino cherries**
- **raisins**

Let each child assemble snack as shown.

Learning Time

Guessing Animals

- **pictures of animals**
- **safety pin or tape**

(1) Attach picture on back of child without showing picture to this child.
(2) The group gives clues, and the child tries to guess the animal. For example, if the animal is a pig, the group might say, "This animal is pink. It has a curly tail. It rolls around in mud."
(3) Limit child to 3 guesses. Let children take turns.

Outdoor Play

Lead the group in a game of Simon Says that uses animal movements. For example, Simon could tell children to scamper like a squirrel, hop like a bunny, slither like a snake, or fly like a bird.

Storytime

See page 7.

Indoor Play

Bring out colorful illustrated books about farm animals.

Art

Fuzzy Animals

- glue
- scissors
- large, precut animal shapes
- variety of soft and furry material, such as yarn, fake fur, felt, cotton

Have children cut and glue fuzzies on animal shapes.

Music

Nursery Rhymes and Songs

"Baa, Baa, Black Sheep"   "Itsy, Bitsy Spider"
"Mary Had a Little Lamb"   "Old MacDonald's Farm"

Snack

Pigs in Blankets

- hot dogs (cut in half)
- refrigerator biscuits

(1) Let each child wrap biscuit dough around a hot dog half and pinch dough edges together.
(2) Bake according to directions on biscuit package.

Learning Time

Lead a discussion about farm animals that have similar qualities. Ask such questions as:

What can fly? (ducks, geese)
What lays eggs? (ducks, geese, chickens)
What has a tail? (cows, pigs, horses)
What has four legs? (cows, pigs, horses)

Outdoor Play

Line Leader

(1) Choose a child to be leader.
(2) Others line up behind leader and copy leader's motions. Suggested motions are jumping, waving arms, skipping, touching toes, somersaults, hopping, and animal movements, such as galloping.

Storytime

Tell or read a story that features farm animals. Ask a children's librarian for suggestions.

Field Trip

Visit to Petting Zoo, Farm, or Pet Store

Discuss each animal's name, what sound it makes, what it eats, and what its offspring are called. If you go to a zoo or pet store, talk about which of the animals found there might live on farms.

Indoor Play

Animal Sounds

(1) Talk about sounds that farm animals make.
(2) Imitate sounds and have the children guess what animal you're imitating.

Music

Sing "Old MacDonald's Farm."

Snack

If you visit a farm, ask whether it would be possible to have some fresh milk!

Learning Time

(1) With the children, act out different farm animal movements. For example, show how:

chickens flap their wings
ducks waddle
goats jump
horses gallop and trot
pigs run, hunch-backed and with short steps
bulls paw and stomp
rabbits hop
kittens climb
turkeys wiggle their necks back and forth

(2) Talk about where different farm animals live: in a pasture, barn, hutch, pen, or laying house.
(3) Ask the group to name some things that farm animals give us: eggs, milk, cheese, wool.

April
Week 3

But I need to go out to make sure this stuff works!

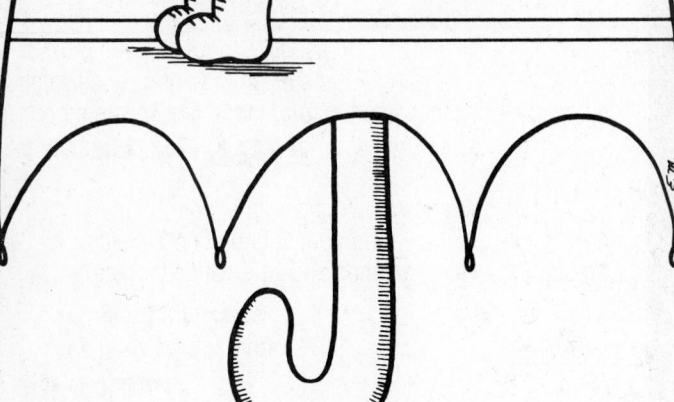

Weather

Indoor Play
Driving in the Snow
- **cookie sheets with sides**
- **salt**
- **small toy cars**

Cover bottom of cookie sheets with salt and let children play with toy cars in the "snow."

Art
Cotton Clouds

- **cotton balls**
- **crayons**
- **construction paper**
- **glue**

Tell children to:
(1) draw a scene on paper, making plenty of sky;
(2) glue on cotton in sky area to resemble clouds.

Music
Hear the Scale
(1) Play a piano or a xylophone, going up and down scales many times. Have the children sing along.
(2) Direct the group to stand up gradually as notes go up the scale and to sit down as notes go down the scale.
(3) Have children motion with their hands to show when the music is going up or down.
(4) Give each child a chance to play the instrument.

Snack
Peeled apples are like snowballs you can eat!

Learning Time
Dictated Umbrella Story

I am in the rain.

- **crayons**
- **construction paper**
- **pencil**

(1) Discuss rainy weather.
(2) Have each child draw a picture of himself or herself in rainy day apparel, leaving space at the bottom of the paper for the dictation.
(3) On the bottom of the paper, write down what the child tells you about the picture.

Outdoor Play
See page 6 for suggested activities.

Storytime
See suggestions on page 7.

Indoor Play
Bring out dolls and doll clothes.

Art
Weather Chart
- paper plates
- crayons
- construction paper arrows
- brass fasteners

Help each child:
(1) divide a plate into 4 sections and in each section draw a symbol from the list below:

| sun | snow or snowman |
| rain or umbrella | clouds |

(2) attach arrow to center of plate with fastener;
(3) point arrow to today's weather.

Music
Finger Plays and Songs

"Five Little Monkeys"	"Here Is the Beehive"
"Jack-in-the-Box"	"Row Your Boat"
"Bingo"	"Pop! Goes the Weasel"

Circle Dances

| "Hokey Pokey" | "Farmer in the Dell" |
| "Ring around the Rosie" | "London Bridge" |

Snack
Use your imagination!

Learning Time
What to Wear
- doll clothes or child's clothes
- weather charts from art lesson

(1) Hold up an article of clothing.
(2) Have children turn the arrows on their weather charts to the appropriate weather conditions for wearing the item.
(3) Repeat step 2 with several more articles of clothing.

Outdoor Play
Try flying kites today!

Storytime
Microphone Fun
Tape a piece of rope to a toilet paper roll. Children can talk into "microphone" as they give weather reports.

Indoor Play
See suggestions on page 3.

Art
Pinwheels
- scissors
- crayons
- tape
- straight pins

- 8″ x 8″ squares of construction paper
- pencils with erasers

Have children follow the steps below to create pinwheels. They will need help with steps 3, 4, and 5.
(1) Color bright designs on both sides of paper.
(2) Fold paper in half diagonally and then fold again.
(3) Open paper, draw a circle (1″ diameter) in middle, and cut on fold lines but not through circle.
(4) Tape right corner of each triangle to the circle.
(5) Insert pin through center of paper, attaching pinwheel to eraser end of pencil.

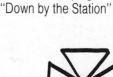

Music
Nursery Rhymes and Songs

| "Little Miss Muffet" | "Are You Sleeping?" |
| "Mary Had a Little Lamb" | "Down by the Station" |

Snack
Children can make pinwheel sandwiches by cutting each sandwich into fourths and arranging them as shown.

Learning Time
Wind
- pinwheels from art lesson
- straw
- paper

(1) Discuss wind and how it feels.
(2) Let children create wind by blowing through a straw and directing it at a piece of paper or hair.
(3) Have them blow into the pinwheel vanes.

Outdoor Play
Have the group take their pinwheels outdoors.

Storytime
Read the poem "Who Has Seen the Wind?" by Christina Rossetti. Also, read other weather poems.

April
Week 4

Teacher, look what I picked just for you!

Growing Things

Indoor Play

Bring out several pairs of shoes of different colors and sizes. Let children mix and match.

Art

See-Through Window

- **leaves and flower petals**
- **waxed paper sandwich bags**
- **iron**

(1) Have children place leaves and petals in waxed paper bags. They should not overlap plants.
(2) The children can watch while you cover each bag with a towel or newspaper and press with hot iron. (The watchword is "safety"!)

Music

Everyone can act out "Plant a Seed" (tune of "Twinkle, Twinkle").

> Now it's time to plant the seed.
> Water, sun, and soil are all I need.
> First some roots and then a stem,
> Then some leaves out on a limb.
> Grow, tree, grow—that's what you do.
> Come climb up on a branch or two.

Snack

Ants on a Log

- **raisins**
- **celery**
- **peanut butter**

(1) Wash and cut celery into small pieces.
(2) Let children fill with peanut butter and place raisins on top.

Learning Time

Celery Absorbs Color

- **celery**
- **food coloring**
- **glass of water**

(1) Have children examine a stalk of celery.
(2) Cut off end of stalk and place celery in water that is tinted with food coloring.
(3) Show the group how, within a few hours, the stalk veins will take in the food coloring, demonstrating the absorption of water. Relate this process to the way roots "drink" water.

Outdoor Play

See page 6 for suggested activities.

Storytime

See page 7 for Storytime suggestions.

Indoor Play
Children can use tongs to lift cotton balls and drop them into a bowl. Then they can count how many they get in.

Art
Seed Design

- **crayons**
- **glue**
- **construction paper**
- **seeds, beans, corn and wheat kernels**

Have each child:
(1) make a simple design on paper;
(2) glue on seeds, beans, and kernels to fill in each section of the design.

Music
Listening to Background Music
(1) Have the group listen to a record that has music and tells a story. Talk about the background music. For example, for the story of Goldilocks, you might ask what the music sounds like when she is walking in the woods, when she breaks the chair, and when the bears come home.
(2) Pick certain parts of the record to play again and ask such questions as:
　　Is this part scary?
　　Is this part happy or sad?
　　How does this music make you feel?

Snack
See page 5.

Learning Time
Carrot Plant

- **carrots**
- **small plastic containers**

(1) Have children break off carrot leaves.
(2) Cut 1″ piece off thick end of each child's carrot.
(3) Child places carrot cut side down in container, fills halfway with water, and places in sun to sprout.

Outdoor Play
See page 6.

Storytime
Story of a Plant
Tell the story of how a seed grows. In the story, incorporate parts of a plant (roots, stems, leaves, flowers) and what makes plants grow.

Field Trip
Nursery or Florist
(1) Tour the seed section of the greenhouse.
(2) Point out the beginning stages of fruits and vegetable plants.
(3) Direct children's attention to the colors and smells.
(4) Buy some flats or a tray of plants to transplant.

Art
Making a Fruit Bowl

- **white playdough (recipe on page 4)**
- **red, orange, and yellow food coloring**

Let each child:
(1) make a small bowl out of white dough;
(2) color small handfuls of playdough, making some red, some orange, and some yellow;
(3) roll colored dough into such fruit shapes as oranges, bananas, and cherries to fill fruit bowl.

Snack
Fresh, raw vegetables make a nutritious snack.

Learning Time
Transplanting Flats

- **plastic cups**
- **plant flat**
- **trowel**
- **spoons**
- **pebbles**

(1) Have each child put hole in bottom of cup, line cup with pebbles, and spoon in small amount of soil.
(2) Use trowel to remove plants from the flat. Insert a plant in each cup.
(3) Let children add more soil and water plants.

Storytime
Have the children recite the rhyme "Mary, Mary, Quite Contrary."

　　Mary, Mary, quite contrary,
　　How does your garden grow?
　　With silver bells and cockleshells
　　And pretty maidens all in a row.

May
Week 1

But I'm just pretending the school is on fire!

Community Workers

Field Trip
A Visit to a Bakery or Pizza Parlor
Call ahead to find out when the cakes are decorated or when dough is made. Plan your trip for that time.

Snack
No-Bake Graham Cookies

- ½ c. dates
- ½ c. raisins
- 2 tbsp. honey
- 3 graham crackers

Children can help:
(1) measure dates, raisins, and honey and pour them into bowl;
(2) crush graham crackers with a rolling pin and add to honey-fruit mixture until dry enough to roll into balls.

Learning Time
Bakery Play

- cookie sheets
- cookie cutters
- measuring cups and spoons
- play money
- cash register or egg carton
- playdough

Children can set up a bakery and take turns being baker, customer, and salesperson.

Indoor Play
See page 3 for suggested activities.

Art
Fire Engine

- precut circular and rectangular shapes
- construction paper
- crayons
- glue

(1) Have children glue precut shapes on paper to resemble fire engines. Make a sample for them to copy.
(2) They can use crayons to add details.

Music
Everyone can sing and act out "The Community Worker Song" (tune of "Farmer in the Dell").

The fire fighters are brave.
The fire fighters are brave.
Heigh-ho, what do you know,
The fire fighters are brave.

Other possible verses:
Barbers cut our hair . . .
Doctors keep us well . . .
Bakers bake our bread . . .

Snack
Fruit Kabob
Have everyone arrange and thread cubed fresh fruit on straws.

Learning Time
Job Charades

- index cards
- box
- pen

(1) Draw a different worker's hat on each card.
(2) Place cards in box. Have a child choose and look at one and then act out the job implied by the picture on the card.
(3) Others try to guess which worker the child is imitating.
(4) Whoever guesses correctly takes a turn.

Outdoor Play
Be a Carpenter
Children can use toy hammers to pound golf tees into styrofoam.

Storytime
See page 7.

Field Trip
Visit to Fire Station
Call ahead to arrange a tour of a fire station. Before visiting, warn the children that the fire fighters might need to leave for a real fire and that the siren is very loud.

Music
Everyone can sing and act out "Fire Fighter" (tune of "Pop! Goes the Weasel").

Down the street the fire fighters go. *(pretend to drive)*
They're off to fight a fire.
Up the ladder with a hose, *(pretend to climb)*
Out goes the fire. *(pretend to squirt a hose)*

Learning Time
Emergency Situations
(1) Have group discuss what they would do in emergency situations. Have them suppose that a fire started at home, a little brother or sister ate some pills, or a friend fell off a bike and couldn't move.
(2) After children express their thoughts, give practical advice about what to do in emergencies.

May
Week 2

DEAR MOMMY,
I MADE YOU A
PRESENT.
I ATE IT.
I LOVE YOU.
Shannon

Mother's Day

Indoor Play

Put in Order
(1) Pair up children and line up 3 or 4 objects on the floor in front of each pair.
(2) Have 1 child cover eyes while other child rearranges objects.
(3) First child tries to put objects in original order.

Art

Flowers for Mom
- construction paper
- scissors
- crayons
- glue
- straws
- paper cups
- sand

Help children:
(1) draw and cut out flower shapes from paper;
(2) glue flowers to top of straws;
(3) fill cup with sand and insert straws.

Music

"My Mom" (tune of "Are You Sleeping?")
My mom's special, my mom's special.
Look and see, Mom and me.
I love her, she loves me.
Lucky me, lucky me.

Snack

Strawberry Stir
- bananas
- strawberries
- milk

Have each child:
(1) mash 4 strawberries and ½ banana in a cup;
(2) add 1 cup milk;
(3) stir vigorously.

Learning Time

A Gift for Mother
With the group, discuss some things they could give as presents to their mothers for Mother's Day. Suggest giving a big hug and kiss, making an original card, or doing a special job or chore.

Outdoor Play

See page 6.

Storytime

See page 7.

Indoor Play

See page 3 for some ideas.

Art

Love to My Toes Card

- construction paper
- crayons
- scissors
- cardboard
- dried or fresh flowers

I love you, Mom, from my head to my toes.

Have each child:

(1) trace footprint on paper, color, and cut out;
(2) on a rectangular piece of cardboard, write *I love you, Mom, from my head to my toes* (you may need to write message for each child);
(3) glue footprint onto cardboard and insert flowers under foot before glue dries.

Music

Body Sounds

(1) Have children experiment with body sounds and movements:

whistling	lip smacking
finger snapping	head nodding
knee knocking	heel clicking
arm flapping	

(2) Play records and have children use body sounds and movements mentioned above.

Snack

Try fresh pineapple with cottage cheese.

Learning Time

Story about Mom

- paper
- pen
- crayons

(1) The group can discuss the special things that their moms do and how happy moms make us feel.
(2) Have children draw pictures about their mothers.
(3) Below each picture, write the special thoughts the child tells you about his or her mom.

Outdoor Play

See how many different kinds of flowers and plants the children can identify.

Storytime

Let the children act out simple nursery rhymes, such as "Jack, Be Nimble," "Jack and Jill," and "Little Miss Muffet."

Indoor Play

Bring out plastic containers and lids. Children can mix and match them.

Art

Bird Feeder Gift

- peanut butter
- birdseed
- yarn
- pinecone or toilet paper roll

Have each child:

(1) dab peanut butter on pinecone or toilet paper roll;
(2) roll it in birdseed and tie on yarn as hanger.

Music

Finger Plays and Songs

"Five Little Monkeys"	"Open, Shut Them"
"Jack-in-the-Box"	"Wheels on the Bus"
"Happy and You Know It"	"Down by the Station"

Circle Dances

"Hokey Pokey"	"Looby Loo"
"Ring around the Rosie"	"Mulberry Bush"

Snack

Each child can spread some tuna salad in a celery stalk.

Learning Time

Acting out "Goldilocks and the Three Bears"

(1) Read or tell the story until the group is very familiar with it.
(2) Let each child choose a part (Mama Bear, Papa Bear, Baby Bear, or Goldilocks).
(3) Read or tell story while children act out parts. They can use imaginary props, facial expressions, and body motions.
(4) Older children can handle speaking parts, using their own words while acting out the story.

Outdoor Play

Playdough Impressions

(1) Make some playdough (recipe on page 4).
(2) Each child can press playdough hard against a textured object such as wood, vents, bark, cement, or leaves.
(3) Others can try to guess which object made each impression.

Storytime

See page 7 for ideas.

May
Week 3

"But I named him and everything!"

Crawly Friends

Indoor Play
Make a batch of playdough (recipe on page 4). The children can form dough into shapes of "crawly friends."

Art
Egg Carton Caterpillar
- cardboard egg cartons
- scissors
- nontoxic paint
- paintbrushes
- marking pens
- pipe cleaners or straws

(1) Cut egg carton bottoms in half lengthwise.
(2) Each child paints a carton half.
(3) When paint dries, child marks face on end of carton and inserts pipe cleaners or straws for feelers.

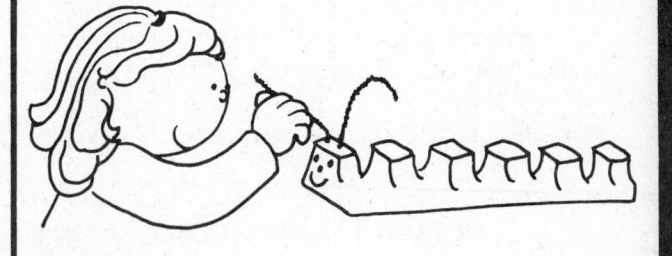

Music
Interpreting Music
(1) Play various kinds of records and have a child interpret the music with motions.
(2) Have others imitate. Let children take turns.

Snack/Learning Time
Butterfly Lunch
- bread
- whole pickles
- lunch meat
- sandwich dressing
- cheese

(1) Children can spread bread with dressing and top with meat, cheese, and another bread slice.
(2) Cut each sandwich into 2 triangles. Each child can arrange triangles around a pickle, as shown.

Outdoor Play
Snail Walk
Children can place snails on dark paper and watch the trails the snails make. Have children wash their hands after handling snails.

Storytime
See page 7.

Indoor Play

See page 3.

Art

Pairs of Triangles

- scissors
- construction paper
- crayons

Have each child:
(1) cut out several pairs of triangles;
(2) write a number on 1 triangle and draw a corresponding number of objects on the other triangle of that pair.

Music

Nursery Rhymes and Songs

"Humpty Dumpty"   "Twinkle, Twinkle"
"Jack and Jill"   "I'm a Little Teapot"
"Baa, Baa, Black Sheep"   "Down by the Station"

Circle Dances

"Mulberry Bush"   "Ring around the Rosie"
"Punchinello"

Snack

See page 5.

Learning Time

Butterfly Match

- clothespins
- pairs of triangles from art lesson

(1) Place triangles on floor.
(2) Have children find each pair of triangles with corresponding numeral and number of drawn objects.
(3) They can clip each pair together with a clothespin to form a butterfly.

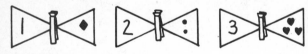

Outdoor Play

Bring out a tub of water and some sponges. Children can create designs with wet sponges on cement.

Storytime

Talk to the Butterflies

Have the group tell stories about their butterflies. Ask such questions as:

   What does your butterfly eat?
   Where has it been?
   What has it seen?

Indoor Play

Curly Patterns

- spiral-curled noodles (uncooked)

(1) Start patterns and have children continue them.
(2) Have the group create designs and shapes.

Art

Potato Raisin Sculpture

- raisins
- potatoes
- toothpicks

Supervise carefully while children:
(1) stick toothpicks in potato;
(2) spear raisins on ends of toothpicks.

Music

Finger Plays and Songs

"Open, Shut Them"   "Five Little Monkeys"
"I've Been Working on the "Itsy, Bitsy Spider"
Railroad"   "Old MacDonald's Farm"

Circle Dances

"Hokey Pokey"   "London Bridge"
"Looby Loo"   "Skip to My Lou"

Snack

Mix yogurt with fruit cocktail and sunflower seeds.

Learning Time

Backyard Science

- plastic margarine tubs and lids

(1) Punch holes in lids.
(2) Lead the group on an exploration in a nearby garden or yard, looking for all sorts of bugs and insects. (An identification book would be helpful.)
(3) Have children capture harmless bugs in the plastic tubs.
(4) Have them observe their bugs for a short while and then let them go.

Outdoor Play

Caterpillar, Caterpillar, Butterfly
Follow rules to Duck, Duck, Goose on page 11.

Storytime

See page 7 for activity ideas.

May
Week 4

Hey, look how big my hand is!

Shapes and Sizes

Indoor Play
Let children play with blocks and balls.

Art
My Shape Book
- crayons
- construction paper
- stapler

square | circle

(1) Tell each child to stack 2-4 pieces of paper and fold them to resemble a book. Staple pages on fold.
(2) Help children print *My Shape Book* on covers.
(3) Help them write names of shapes, such as rectangle, triangle, star, oval, diamond, and hexagon. They can then draw shapes on pages and color them.

Music
Nursery Rhymes and Songs

"Jack and Jill"   "Baa, Baa, Black Sheep"
"This Old Man"   "Hickory, Dickory Dock"

Snack
See page 5.

Learning Time
Musical Motions
(1) Give paper and crayon to each child.
(2) The children sing and draw with large arm movements to the song "Musical Motions" (tune of Mulberry Bush").
    Round and round and round we go.
    Round and round and round we go.
    Round and round and round we go.
    Where we stop, nobody knows.
(3) Repeat step 2 using words "down and up and down" and "side to side to side" in song.

Outdoor Play
Bubbles
- ½ c. liquid dishwashing soap
- ½ c. water
- plastic straws

(1) Mix water and soap.
(2) At 1 end of each straw, cut 4 slits about 1" long. Bend strips back.
(3) Children can dip straws into bubble solution and enjoy blowing bubbles. Supervise carefully.

Storytime
See page 7.

Indoor Play
See page 3 for some suggestions.

Art
Playdough Shapes

- plastic knives
- playdough (recipe on page 4)

Have children flatten playdough with hand or roller and use knives to cut shapes.

Music
Circle Dance

Add movement directions to the last line of "Ring around the Rosie." Everyone sings and acts out:

We all touch our toes!
. . . clap our hands!
. . . snap our fingers!
. . . stamp our feet!

Snack
Finger Gelatin

- 12 oz. frozen apple or grape juice (thawed)
- 3 envelopes unflavored gelatin
- 1½ c. hot water

Prepare gelatin ahead of time, as directed on page 10.

Learning Time
Feeling Bag

- paper bag
- assorted shapes, such as a ball (for a circle), a block (for a square), a domino (for a rectangle)

(1) Place 1 object in the bag. Have a child reach in and feel it.
(2) Have child name the object and its shape.
(3) Alternate objects and let children take turns.

Outdoor Play
Triangle, Triangle, Square

Follow rules to Duck, Duck, Goose on page 11.

Storytime
Have children point out shapes in picture books. Ask them whether they see a circle on a certain page, a square, and other shapes.

Indoor Play
See page 3.

Art
Plate of Shapes

- construction paper
- scissors
- paper plates
- crayons
- glue
- brass fasteners

(1) Have each child choose 4 different shapes (triangle, circle, rectangle, square, diamond, oval, hexagon) and cut 2 of each from construction paper.
(2) Child draws lines to divide plate into 8 wedges.
(3) Child glues shapes on plate (1 per wedge).
(4) Cut out construction paper arrows and attach 2 in center of each plate with fastener.
(5) Have children point arrows to matching pairs.

Music
Finger Plays and Songs

"Teasing Mr. Crocodile"   "Pop! Goes the Weasel"
"Where is Thumbkin?"   "Old MacDonald's Farm"

Circle Dances

"Punchinello"   "Ring around the Rosie"

Snack
Let children help prepare a leafy vegetable salad.

Learning Time
Shape Tune

(1) Pass out geometric shapes. Everyone can sing and act out "Shape Tune" (tune of "Mulberry Bush").
    Do you have the triangle, the triangle, the triangle?
    If you have the triangle, please stand up.
(2) Mention a different shape in each verse. Continue until all the shapes have been named.
(3) Everyone can trade shapes and sing the verses again.

Outdoor Play
Obstacle Course

Set up an obstacle course with opportunities for the children to climb, crawl, run, jump, swing, and so on. The children take turns completing the course.

Storytime
See page 7.

June
Week 1

My Family

Indoor Play
Kitchen Helper

- rags
- sponges
- toy dishes
- dishwashing detergent
- tub

Fill sink or plastic tub with water and soap. Allow children to wash and dry dishes. Supervise play.

Art
Magazine Families

- paper plates
- marking pens
- magazines
- glue
- scissors

(1) Help each child write *My Family* on plate.
(2) Children look through magazines to find pictures of faces resembling those of family members.
(3) Children can tear or cut out pictures and glue them onto paper plates.

Music
Everyone can say poem "My Family" and hold up a finger for each family member.

> This is my mother, so sweet and nice.
> This is my father, who hugs me twice.
> This is my brother, so big and tall.
> This is my sister, who's still quite small.
> This is the baby, so little, you see.
> All different sizes in this family.

Snack
Mix yogurt and fresh fruit.

Learning Time
Playing House

- assorted props, such as toy furniture and dress-up clothes

(1) Set up a household situation, such as a new baby in the house, dinner guests, a new babysitter, a child's birthday.
(2) Let children choose roles and act out the situation. Have them take turns playing roles.

Outdoor Play
See page 6.

Storytime
Each child shares a story about a favorite family outing.

Indoor Play

See page 3.

Art

Body Prints

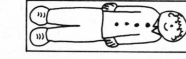

- **crayons**
- **large pieces of paper**

Have children:

(1) lie down on top of paper while partner traces around her or his body;
(2) use crayons to draw clothes and facial features.

Music

Everyone can sing and act out "Daddy in the Dell" (tune of "Farmer in the Dell").

The daddy in the house,
The daddy in the house,
Heigh-ho the derry-o,
The daddy in the house.

Other verses:

The daddy takes a mommy . . .
The mommy takes a daughter . . .
The daughter takes a brother . . .
The brother takes a baby . . .

Snack

Frozen Banana

- **bananas**
- **Popsicle sticks**

(1) Let children peel bananas.
(2) Cut bananas in half.
(3) Give a half to each child and let children place bananas on Popsicle sticks.
(4) Freeze bananas.

Learning Time

This Is My Family

(1) Have each child talk into a tape recorder and tell about each member of her or his family. Some children might like to imitate family members.
(2) Replay the recording for everyone to hear.

Outdoor Play

Flying Disc

Cut the center out of some plastic lids and let children play catch or ring a bottle with them.

Storytime

Share experiences that you remember from your childhood.

Field Trip

Visiting People at Work

(1) Take the group to visit a person (possibly a child's parent) at work. Call ahead to make specific plans.
(2) If possible, have the worker speak briefly with the children about his or her work.

Snack

Pickled Carrot Sticks

- **carrot sticks**
- **sweet pickle juice**

Place carrot sticks in juice for half an hour. These are great for taking along on field trips!

Learning Time

Family Portraits

- **slide projector**
- **family slides**
- **photo albums**

(1) Show slides or pictures from albums.
(2) Let children narrate their pictures. They can name the people and tell about the events portrayed in each picture.

June
Week 2

Alphabet

Indoor Play
See page 3.

Art
Letter Puzzles

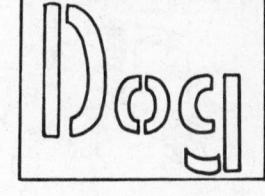

- **precut big and little half circles, curved and straight lines**
- **glue**
- **construction paper**

(1) The children can form letters from shapes, imitating samples you have prepared.
(2) After playing with shapes, they can glue letters they made from the shapes on paper.

Music
Nursery Rhymes and Songs

"Jack and Jill"	"Row Your Boat"
"Jack, Be Nimble"	"Teddy Bear"
"Hickory, Dickory Dock"	"Bingo"

Circle Dances

"Hokey Pokey"	"Ring around the Rosie"
"Skip to My Lou"	

Snack
Peanut Butter Banana

- **bananas**	- **rolling pin**
- **graham crackers**	- **plastic knives**
- **peanut butter**	- **waxed paper**
- **paper bag**	- **stapler**

(1) Put several graham crackers in paper bag, fold down top, and staple shut.
(2) Let children take turns crushing crackers with rolling pin.
(3) Children can peel bananas, cut them in half, and spread them with peanut butter.
(4) Let children pour crushed crackers onto waxed paper and roll banana in crumbs.

Learning Time
Chalkboard Writing
Slowly print children's names on the chalkboard. Have them say the letters. Let children experiment with chalk and attempt to write their names.

Outdoor Play
Sandwriting
Children can write letters in sand with finger or stick.

Storytime
See page 7.

Indoor Play
Salt Box Writing
- **shoe box lid**
- **dark colored construction paper**
- **salt**

Press paper into box lid. Pour in salt. Have children use fingers to print letters in salt. Shake lid to "erase."

Art
Clay Letters
(1) Make a batch of clay (recipe on page 4).
(2) Let each child pull off a 1½" ball of dough.
(3) Children can roll dough into ropes and form letters.
(4) Place letters on cookie sheet and bake them at 350° until light brown. Children should NOT eat the letters.

Music
Songs
"I've Been Working on the Railroad"

"Yankee Doodle"

"Five Little Monkeys"

Circle Dances
"London Bridge"

"Punchinello"

Snack
Cook and butter alphabet macaroni. Serve with cheese.

Learning Time
Meaningful Squiggles
- **crayons**
- **paper**

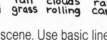

bunny hopped   tall grass   clouds rolling   rain came

(1) Tell a short story or describe a scene. Use basic lines and circles to illustrate the story. For example:
> One day the bunny hopped across the tall grass. She saw the clouds rolling in the sky and soon the rain came.

(2) Have children copy your illustrations while you repeat the story.
(3) Let the children create their own stories.

Outdoor Play
Take a walk with the group. Have them look for addresses (building numbers, street names). Let children talk about their addresses.

Storytime
Read or tell the story of Pinocchio.

Indoor Play
The group can use magnetic letters on any metal surface.

Art
Rainbow Sandpaper Letters
- **sandpaper**
- **crayons**
- **construction paper**
- **iron**
- **scissors**

(1) Have children draw letters on sandpaper, coloring solidly and using several different colors.
(2) Place a piece of paper on top of colored sandpaper and press briefly with warm iron. Letters will transfer to construction paper. (Letters—except A, H, I, M, O, T, U, V, W, X, and Y—will be backwards.)
(3) Children can cut out sandpaper letters.

Music
Songs
"Alphabet Song" (see page 16)

"I'm a Little Teapot"

"Old MacDonald's Farm"

"Bingo"

"Yankee Doodle"

"Where Is Thumbkin?"

Musical Chairs
Follow the directions on page 30.

Snack
Strawberry Smash
- **toast**
- **peanut butter**
- **strawberries**

Each child can:
(1) wash and stem a strawberry and smash it with a fork;
(2) spread peanut butter and strawberry on toast.

Learning Time
Fishing for Letters
- **magnet**
- **bucket**
- **sandpaper letters from art lesson**
- **paper clips**
- **string**
- **dowel or stick**

(1) Attach string to dowel and magnet to end of string. Place a paper clip on each letter.
(2) Have children put all the letters in bucket and take turns fishing. They can say the name of each letter they catch.

Outdoor Play
Children can practice writing letters with chalk on the cement. The chalk will wash off with water.

Storytime
See page 7.

June
Week 3

Dear daddy,
Momy bought you A watch
four Fathers day, its a
secret so dont tell
any body, you are a supper
dad, you are grate.
Love Spencer.

Father's Day

Indoor Play

Hide the Clock

(1) Children take turns hiding a ticking alarm clock.

(2) Other children listen carefully and look for clock.

Art

"Leather" Pencil Holder

- small jars or cans
- masking tape
- shoe polish
- rags

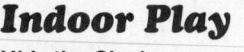

Have each child:

(1) tear off small strips of tape and place over the entire outside of the jar;

(2) rub some polish on tape to create a leatherlike appearance.

Music

Finger Plays and Songs

"Five in the Bed"   "Wheels on the Bus"

"Jack-in-the-Box"   "Are You Sleeping?"

"Here Is the Beehive"   "Row Your Boat"

Snack

Orange-Banana Shake

- orange juice
- bananas
- milk

Each child can:

(1) smash a banana in a jar;

(2) add ¼ cup orange juice and ½ cup milk;

(3) put lid on jar and shake.

Learning Time

A Gift for Father

(1) Begin a story about a child who doesn't have any money to buy a gift for Father's Day.

(2) Have children complete the story by telling different ways the child could still say "Happy Father's Day," such as making a card, doing an extra job, or giving a hug and a kiss.

Outdoor Play

Balloon Tetherball

Tie a balloon to a string. Attach string to a post. Children can hit balloon back and forth.

Storytime

See page 7.

Indoor Play
Drop It

(1) Arrange assorted items on a tray, such as a ball, keys, spoons.
(2) Ask children to look carefully at items on tray.
(3) Choose a child to be IT. While other children cover their eyes, IT drops an item on floor and returns it to the tray.
(4) Others take turns guessing what was dropped.

Art
Decorated Tins

- **coffee tins with lids**
- **aluminum foil**
- **macaroni**
- **glue**

(1) Have children cover coffee tins with foil.
(2) They can decorate lids by gluing macaroni on top.

Music
Musical Relays

(1) Have the group stand in a line. They pass a ball to each other in various ways (overhead, through legs, and so on) while a record plays.
(2) When you stop the music, the child holding the ball is "caught" and must sit out until the next game.
(3) Game continues until only 1 player remains. Then start over.

Snack/Learning Time
Father's Peanut Treat

- **2 qts. popped popcorn**
- **1 c. salted peanuts**
- **1 tbsp. butter**
- **1 c. molasses**
- **½ c. brown sugar**
- **candy thermometer**

(1) Cook butter, sugar, and molasses until candy thermometer reads 280°.
(2) Add popcorn and peanuts, coating them evenly. Spread mixture on cookie sheet.
(3) Let children shape cooled mixture into small balls.
(4) They can fill decorated tins from art lesson to make Father's Day gifts.

Outdoor Play
See page 6.

Storytime
Talk about how to care for books properly.

Indoor Play
Each child can draw a page of happy faces for her or his dad.

Art
Tie Card

- **construction paper**
- **assorted wrapping ribbons**
- **scissors**
- **glue**

Each child can:
(1) fold a piece of paper in half to make a card;
(2) cut out a tie shape from contrasting paper;
(3) glue tie on front of card and write *To Daddy*;
(4) use ribbon to decorate tie.

Music
See page 5.

Snack
Daddy Longlegs

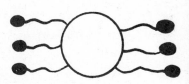

- **peach halves**
- **grape halves**
- **cooked spaghetti**

Help children prepare their snacks as shown.

Learning Time
Writing to Dad

- **pen**
- **tie cards from art lesson**

(1) Discuss what is special about fathers and how happy they make us feel.
(2) Have each child dictate some special thoughts about his or her father. Write them inside the card and sign child's name or have child personalize the card.

Outdoor Play
Father May I

(1) Choose a child to be FATHER. Have other children stand along side of play area opposite FATHER.
(2) One by one, children ask FATHER whether they can take a specific number of steps forward. FATHER responds, "Yes, you may" or "No, you may not."
(3) Children continue taking turns and walking toward FATHER. The first child to reach FATHER becomes the new FATHER, and the game begins again.

Storytime
What If? Story
Begin story: "What if I turned into a mouse and lived in someone's house?" Let children take turns adding to story.

June
Week 4

Summer

Indoor Play
Spin the Bottle
(1) Children sit in a circle facing each other. Place an empty plastic bottle in the middle of the circle.
(2) Let a child spin the bottle. When the bottle stops spinning, the child at whom it is pointing sings a song or does a trick.
(3) The group keeps playing until everyone has had a turn.

Learning Time
Summer Walk
(1) Take the group on a walk to look for signs of summer.
(2) Everyone can collect "treasures," such as leaves and flowers, in paper bags.

Music
The group can sing and act out "What Do We Like to Do in the Summer?" (tune of "Mulberry Bush").

What do we like to do in the summer,
Do in the summer, do in the summer?
What do we like to do in the summer
To have a lot of fun?
We swim a lot in the swimming pool,
In the swimming pool, in the swimming pool.
We swim a lot in the swimming pool,
And this is how it's done.

Other verses:
We build sand castles at the beach . . .
We eat good food at barbecues . . .

Snack
Serve cool melon slices.

Art
Summer Collage
- **paper plates**
- **marking pen**
- **glue**
- **bag with treasures from summer walk**

(1) Help children title their plates *Summer*.
(2) They can glue collected objects onto plates.

Outdoor Play
Have children bring bathing suits to wear. If weather permits, turn on the sprinklers or a hose for water play.

Storytime
Children can take turns telling what they like best about the summer months.

Indoor Play
See page 3.

Art
Lemonade Sign

- large piece of plain cardboard
- color markers or crayons

(1) Print *Lemonade for Sale* in outline form for children.
(2) Have children color in letters and decorate sign with lemons.

Music
Feeling Vibrations

(1) Have children sing songs, touching their throats to feel the vibrations.
(2) Have them sing songs into small, empty raisin boxes, feeling the box bottoms for vibrations.

Snack
Lemonade

- 1 c. sugar
- 1 c. water
- 4 c. cold water
- ¾ c. lemon juice (4–6 lemons, squeezed)
- ice

(1) Boil 1 cup water and sugar for 5 minutes. Cool.
(2) Let children mix remaining ingredients.

Learning Time
Lemonade for Sale

- lemonade sign from art lesson
- card table
- tape
- paper cups
- napkins
- trash bag
- egg carton or toy cash register
- play money or pennies
- lemonade from snacktime

(1) Tape lemonade sign to table.
(2) Have children help set up lemonade stand outside.
(3) The children can take turns selling, pouring, and buying lemonade.

Outdoor Play
If it's a warm day, let children play with spray bottles filled with water.

Storytime
What If? Story

Let the group take turns completing a story that begins: "What if a bear came into my tent while I was camping out in my very own backyard?"

Field Trip
Visit to the Beach or Lake

(1) Show children samples of seaweed, driftwood, shells, and other water-related objects. Have children share buckets and collect items together.
(2) Give children paper cups. Let them sit at the edge of the water and try to catch small water animals or floating plants. Supervise water play carefully.
(3) Children can have fun making body prints and trails in the sand.

Art
Shell Monsters

- shells
- glue
- tempera paints
- paintbrushes
- newspaper

Have children:
(1) spread newspaper out on table;
(2) glue shells together to form monsters or other creatures;
(3) let glue dry and then paint creatures.

Snack
Fruity Fruit Cubes

- fruit juice
- small pieces of fresh fruit
- ice cube tray

(1) Pour juice into ice cube tray.
(2) Let children drop a piece of fruit into each section.
(3) Freeze the juice cubes.

July
Week 1

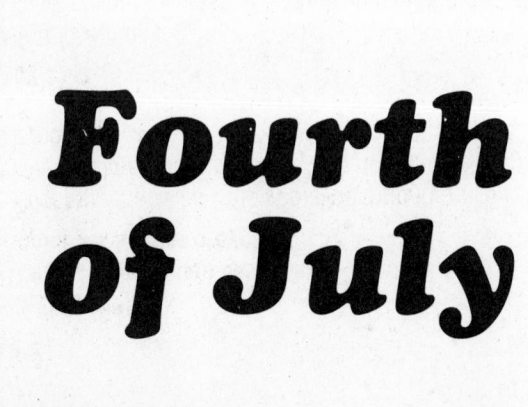

I didn't know how to make stars, so I made moons instead. OK?

Fourth of July

Indoor Play
The group can build towers with blocks. Have them count how many blocks they use and knock down the blocks.

Art
United States Flag
- **red and blue paper**
- **large white paper**
- **star stickers**
- **scissors**
- **dowel**
- **tape**
- **glue**

As a group, the children can:
(1) tear or cut red strips of paper and a large blue square;
(2) glue strips and square onto white paper to make a flag;
(3) stick stars on blue paper;
(4) tape flag to dowel.

Music
Sing "Happy Birthday, United States."

Snack
Watermelon slices will refresh children on a warm day.

Learning Time
The Flag
- **flag from art lesson**
- **record of marching music**
- **record player**
- **book with pictures of national flags**

(1) Discuss the importance of a nation's flag.
(2) Explain what the colors and shapes represent.
(3) You may wish to show pictures of other nations' flags.
(4) Play music. Let children march and wave flag.

Outdoor Play
See page 6.

Storytime
Talk with the group about fears, especially a fear of loud noises. Begin to tell a story about a child afraid of loud fireworks on the Fourth of July. Have each child give a version of the story ending.

Indoor Play

See page 3.

Art

Fourth of July Aprons

- **heavy paper napkins**
- **stapler**
- **ribbon**
- **marking pens**

Children can:

(1) decorate napkins and staple several on ribbon;

(2) wear apron and pull off napkins as they get dirty!

Music

Everyone can sing along with records of patriotic songs.

Snack

Red, White, and Blue Salad

- **strawberries**
- **blueberries**
- **bananas (sliced)**

Children can mix ingredients and serve.

Learning Time

How I Spend the Fourth of July

- **paper**
- **crayons**
- **pen**

(1) With the group, talk about family traditions. Let children tell how they spend the Fourth of July.

(2) Have each child draw a picture about the holiday. Write what the child tells you about the picture.

Outdoor Play

Help the children decorate bikes, trikes, and wagons with red, white, and blue streamers and balloons. Have a parade!

Storytime

Fill-In Story

Tell a story, leaving open-ended similes for children to complete. Encourage children to use their imaginations. For example: "The Fourth of July is finally here. The sun is as hot as ___ . All the children are running around like ___ . The fireworks make noises like ___ ."

Field Trip

Historic Site

(1) Call ahead to arrange a tour of a state or national historic monument, such as a restored building, the site of an important historic event, or a museum.

(2) Try to get a group tour of a government building, such as the city hall, courthouse, or library, or take the group to a city park.

(3) Talk about the history of your town.

Art

Fireworks

- **paper**
- **3–4 colors of watercolor paint**
- **straws**

(1) Drop a small amount of paint in center of each child's paper.

(2) Child blows through straw to create fireworks pattern on paper.

Music

Songs

"Yankee Doodle"

Snack

Popcorn and fruit juice should be a big hit.

July
Week 2

Space

Indoor Play
The group can use playdough to shape stars, planets, suns, moons, rockets, and space people.

Art
Space Picture

- **crayons**
- **paper**
- **black paint**
- **brushes**

(1) Have each child color a night picture with stars, moon, and planets. Make sure they color solidly.
(2) Help them brush black paint over entire picture.

Music
Finger Plays and Songs

"Jack-in-the-Box"   "Are You Sleeping?"
"Here Is the Beehive"   "Twinkle, Twinkle"
"Wheels on the Bus"   "Open, Shut Them"

Circle Dances

"Looby Loo"   "Mulberry Bush"

Snack
Moon Crackers

- **round crackers**
- **cheese spread**

(1) Help children spread cheese on crackers.
(2) Have children take bite of "full moon," then "half moon," and "quarter moon." Explain "new (no) moon."

Learning Time
Day or Night

- **precut suns and moons**

(1) Give each child a sun and a moon.
(2) Have children hold up sun or moon to answer such questions as:
    When do you eat breakfast?
    When do you wear your pajamas?
    When do you ride a bike?
    When do you see stars?

Outdoor Play
Have children make paper airplanes and fly them.

Storytime
What If? Story
Begin story: "What if I took a rocket to the moon?" Let each child add to the story.

Indoor Play
Group can use Tinkertoys to make rockets and satellites.

Art
Space Masks

- large paper plates
- scissors
- large paper bags
- glue
- crayons

Help each child:

(1) cut out rectangle from center of plate;
(2) glue plate on front of bag and cut out part of bag that shows through;
(3) decorate bag with crayon drawings.

Music
Everyone can sing and hold up fingers to act out "Ten Little Space Creatures" (tune of "Ten Little Indians").

One little, two little, three little space creatures,
Four little, five little, six little space creatures,
Seven little, eight little, nine little space creatures,
Ten little space creatures flying. *(wave fingers)*

Snack
Banana Rocket

- bananas (cut in half, as shown)
- pineapple rings
- raisins

Each child can place rocket (banana) in launching pad (pineapple ring) and add raisins.

Learning Time
Riding in a Rocket

- space masks from art lesson
- large, shallow box
- heavy paper plate
- marking pen
- brass fastener
- flashlights

(1) Draw dials on inside of box.
(2) With fastener, attach paper plate to inside of large box. Children use plate as steering wheel.
(3) Children take turns "riding in space." Darken play area and have other children hold flashlights, pretending to be stars.

Outdoor Play
Group can take rocket outdoors for additional rides.

Storytime
See page 7.

Indoor Play
See page 3.

Art
Outer Space

- black paper
- star stickers
- chalk

Children can stick stars on paper and draw moon with chalk.

Music
Play records. Have children be "dancing stars."

Snack
Pudding Sticks

- instant pudding and milk
- paper cups
- Popsicle sticks

(1) Prepare pudding and pour into each cup.
(2) Half-freeze pudding. Children can insert sticks.
(3) When completely frozen, children can tear off paper cups and eat pudding.

Learning Time
Spatial Relationships

- flannel board (see page 7)
- precut shapes of cloud, sun, moon, ringed-planet, star

Let children place shapes on board and tell spatial relationships, using such words as *under* and *over*.

Outdoor Play
See page 6.

Storytime
Little Red Rocket

- flannel board
- precut shapes from Learning Time
- rocket shape cut out of red paper

(1) Begin story: "Little Red Rocket *(place rocket on board)* wanted to get its mother a special surprise—a diamond in the sky. Red Rocket blasted into space and came to a cloud. *(place cloud on board)* 'Are you a diamond in the sky?' asked the Red Rocket. 'No, I'm a cloud,' answered the cloud."
(2) Continue story in this manner, adding sun, moon, and planet to board. Complete story as follows: "Finally, the rocket came to a star who answered, 'Yes, I am a diamond in the sky. I'm also called a star.' *(add star to board and move rocket so nose touches star)* And Red Rocket brought the star home to its mother."

Summer Fun

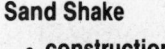

Paper Plate Fish

- **marking pens**
- **paper plates**
- **glue**
- **scissors**

Help each child:
(1) draw and cut out a triangle from plate;
(2) glue triangle to back of plate as shown and draw on extra features.

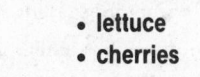

Banana Boat Salad

- **bananas**
- **jam or jelly**
- **cottage cheese**
- **lettuce**
- **cherries**

Help each child:
(1) peel a banana and use a plastic knife to cut banana in half;
(2) place banana on lettuce leaves in a bowl;
(3) top with cottage cheese, jam, and a cherry.

Sand Shake

- **construction paper**
- **glue**
- **sand**

You can use this art project to reinforce lessons in writing letters or numbers. Help each child:
(1) drip glue on paper to make letters, numbers, or a design;
(2) sprinkle sand over paper and shake off excess.

Sandwich Sailboats

- **hot dog buns (separated)**
- **tuna salad**
- **lettuce leaves**
- **plastic straws**

(1) Use a sharp knife to cut out inside of buns, ½" from edges. Be careful not to cut through bottoms.
(2) Let children fill buns with tuna salad.
(3) Help each child thread straw through lettuce leaf and place in tuna salad to make a sail.

Water Scene

- **construction paper**
- **liquid starch**
- **sand**
- **weeds**
- **colorful tissue paper**
- **scissors**
- **brushes**

(1) Cut small fish shapes out of tissue paper.
(2) Help children brush starch all over construction paper, sprinkle sand at bottom of paper, and shake off excess.
(3) Help them place weeds and fish on paper.

Fruit Kabobs

Let each child thread 3 or 4 chunks of fruit on a thin plastic straw.

Target Practice

Children can use spray bottles filled with water to shoot at targets.

Ice Cream Cone Clowns

- **ice cream**
- **ice cream cones**
- **paper baking cups**
- **cherries, nuts, and chocolate bits**

(1) Scoop ice cream into each cup.
(2) Let each child place cone "hat" upside down on scoop of ice cream.
(3) Children can make facial features with cherries, nuts, and chocolate bits.

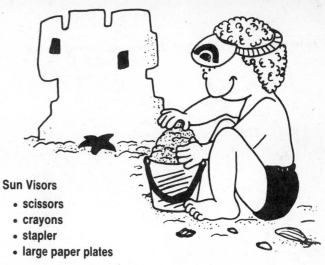

Sun Visors

- **scissors**
- **crayons**
- **stapler**
- **large paper plates**

Help each child:
(1) cut out circle from center of plate, large enough so ring will fit on head;
(2) cut inside circle in half and staple to outside of ring;
(3) decorate visor with crayons.

Blowfish

- **paper lunch bags**
- **marking pens**
- **rubber bands**

(1) Have children draw fish faces on bottoms of bags.
(2) Blow up bags and secure ends with rubber bands.

Postcard Stories

Save vacation postcards. Use them as props while telling stories.

More Summer Fun

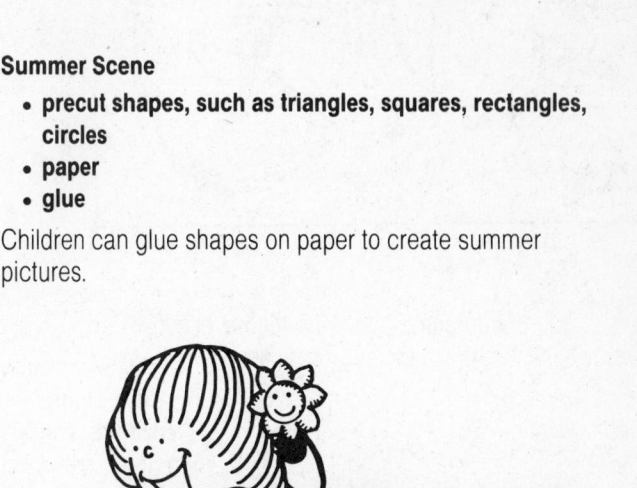

Summer Scene
- **precut shapes, such as triangles, squares, rectangles, circles**
- **paper**
- **glue**

Children can glue shapes on paper to create summer pictures.

Pull Train
Help children connect shoe boxes with a cord or string. Add an extra piece for a handle. Children can decorate boxes.

Watermelon on a Stick
- **1 c. seedless watermelon pieces**
- **1 c. orange juice**
- **1 c. water**
- **paper cups**
- **Popsicle sticks**

Mix ingredients in blender. Pour into paper cups and insert Popsicle sticks when partially frozen. Finish freezing.

Game of Left or Right
Toss a ball or balloon to a player while you call out a command, such as "left foot," "left shoulder," "right hand," or "right knee." The player tries to hit the ball with the body part that you call out.

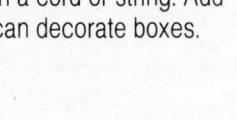

Punching Bag

- **large paper bag**
- **newspaper**
- **string**

(1) Let children fill bag halfway with crumpled newspaper.
(2) Twist bag shut. Tie end of bag with string and hang bag from hook or tree limb.
(3) Children can take turns punching the bag.

Piñata

- **large, heavy paper bag**
- **small boxes of raisins**
- **string**
- **plastic baseball bat**

(1) Put raisins in bag.
(2) Twist bag shut. Tie end with string and hang bag from hook or tree limb.
(3) Children can take turns hitting bag with bat until bag breaks open. Each child gets a box of raisins.

Can You Do This?

Children can take turns being the leader. The leader sings the song "Can You Do This?" (tune of "Are You Sleeping?"), making a different motion for each verse. The others imitate the leader.

> Can you do this? Can you do this?
> Look at me, look at me.
> Everybody try it, everybody try it.
> You will see, you will see.

House in the Forest

- **large paper bags**
- **crayons or marking pens**

Have each child:
(1) tear out "door" from bottom of bag, as shown;
(2) draw windows and doors on bag;
(3) stand bag up on grass and pretend it's a house in the forest.

August
Week 3

Did you know that grape juice and orange curtains make brown?

Colors

Indoor Play
Sorting Colors

- toys
- boxes
- crayons

(1) Label each box a different color by coloring the box or putting a colored label on it.
(2) Have children sort toys by dominant color into boxes.

Art
Color Wheels

- paper plates
- crayons
- brass fasteners
- construction paper
- scissors

(1) Draw 8 wedge-shaped sections on each child's plate.
(2) Have children color each section a different color.
(3) Cut out arrows and help each child attach an arrow to center of plate with brass fastener.

Music
Suggested Record Fun
Play records and have children sing and dance along, move to the rhythm, clap to the beat, practice marching, and wave streamers or scarves to the music.

Snack
Tasty Pineapple Juice

- 32 oz. pineapple juice
- small pkg. of punch-flavored powdered drink mix
- 5 c. water
- ice cubes

Let the children help mix ingredients and add ice cubes.

Learning Time
Color Wheel Game
Let children take turns spinning their color wheels from the art lesson, each time pointing to an object of the same color indicated by the arrow.

Outdoor Play
Have the group play Color Wheel game outdoors.

Storytime
See page 7.

Indoor Play

Scribble Tablecloth

- marking pens
- tape
- shelf paper or butcher paper

(1) Cover a table with several layers of paper and tape paper down.
(2) Let the group create designs on paper with marking pens. Use this paper as a tablecloth during snacktime.

Art

Blending Colors

- paper towels
- 1" water in 4 small bowls
- food coloring (4 colors)

(1) Make each bowl of water a different color. Use several drops of food coloring.
(2) Let each child fold a paper towel twice, as shown, dip each corner of towel in a different color, open towel, and watch colors blend.

Music

Songs

"Apples Are Red" (tune of "Farmer in the Dell")
    Apples and cherries are red.
    The sky and sea are blue.
    Grass and trees and leaves are green.
    I see orange, do you? *(point to orange object)*
Repeat song, inserting different colors.

Snack/Learning Time

Orange Drink

- 6 oz. frozen orange juice
- 1⅓ c. nonfat dry milk
- ¼ tsp. vanilla
- 1 qt. water
- 6-8 ice cubes

Mix ingredients in blender, adding 1 ice cube at a time. Let children help pour drink into cups.

Outdoor Play

See page 6.

Storytime

Select a book with colorful illustrations. Read the story. Then show the pictures again. Point out different colors. Ask, "Where is green? What object is red?" and so on.

Indoor Play

See page 3.

Art

Color Book

- construction paper
- crayons
- magazines
- scissors
- stapler
- glue

(1) Have each child stack and fold in half 2-6 pieces of paper.
(2) Staple each book on the fold.
(3) Have children draw a different color border on each page.
(4) Have children cut pictures of various colors out of magazines and glue pictures on corresponding pages.

Music

Finger Plays

"Open, Shut Them"   "Where Is Thumbkin?"
"Here Is the Beehive"   "Two Little Blackbirds"

Circle Dances

"London Bridge"   "Farmer in the Dell"

Snack

Make popcorn, adding a few drops of food coloring to oil.

Learning Time

Mixing Colors

- 6 clear glasses
- food coloring
- water

Chidren can help or just watch.
(1) Fill 3 glasses with ½ cup water each.
(2) Add several drops of food coloring to each glass and stir. Make a deep red, a yellow, and a blue.
(3) Into other glasses, stir 2 colors together to make a new color.
    yellow + red = orange
    blue + yellow = green
    red + blue = purple

Outdoor Play

Ladder Walk

(1) Using chalk, draw a ladder on the ground.
(2) Have children jump, run, hop, and walk backward up and down the ladder.

Storytime

Tell the story of Rumpelstiltskin.

August
Week 4

ACTIVITY UNIT 1

Indoor Play
See page 3.

Art
Seven Balloons

- **small, precut circles (7 per child)**
- **construction paper**
- **crayons**
- **glue**

Help each child:
(1) place hand on paper and trace 4 fingers, then place hand on paper again and trace 3 fingers;
(2) glue 7 circles at top of paper;
(3) draw a line connecting each circle to a finger.

Snack
Blend fresh fruit and fruit juice for a refreshing drink.

Learning Time
Days of the Week Hop

- **7 paper plates**

(1) Label each plate with a day of the week and tape plates on the floor in order, starting with Sunday.
(2) Children can take turns walking from plate to plate as they sing "Days of the Week" (tune of "Are You Sleeping?").
> Walk when I say every weekday,
> Here we go, don't say no.
> Sunday, Monday, Tuesday,
> Wednesday, Thursday, Friday,
> Saturday—let's all play!

Outdoor Play/Music
Who's Sitting on It Now?

- **small object (coin or button)**

(1) Choose a child to be IT. IT covers eyes.
(2) All others are seated; 1 player sits on object.
(3) IT uncovers eyes and tries to guess who is sitting on object. Children are singing "Who's Sitting on It Now?" (tune of "Farmer in the Dell").
> Who's sitting on it now? Who's sitting on it now?
> Can you guess? Oh, can you guess?
> Who's sitting on it now?
(4) As IT gets closer to the object, children sing louder. As IT gets farther away, children sing softer.
(5) After IT guesses who is sitting on object, choose a new IT and play again.

Storytime
See page 7.

Indoor Play
Calendar Toss

Place large calendar on floor. Children take turns tossing button or coin on numbers or days of the week. Help children read date on which button lands.

Art
"My Best Week Ever" Book

- **construction paper**
- **stapler**
- **marking pens or crayons**

(1) Have each child stack and fold in half 4 pieces of paper.
(2) Staple each book on fold.
(3) Print title *My Best Week Ever* on cover and a day of the week on each page.
(4) Children can draw a favorite activity on each page.

Music
Everyone can sing and march to "Twelve Months" (tune of "Row Your Boat").

Twelve months make a year, sing along with me.
Sing it once and then again, we'll sing it merrily.
January, February, March, and April, too,
May and June and then July—there's still five more, it's true.
August, September, October—the year is almost done.
November and December—I know every one.

Snack
Frozen Peanutty Banana

- **bananas (cut in half)**
- **peanut butter (at room temperature)**
- **Popsicle sticks**
- **granola**

Help each child:
(1) insert Popsicle stick lengthwise into banana;
(2) spread peanut butter with plastic knife on banana and roll it in granola.
Freeze bananas until ready to eat.

Learning Time
Which Month Is Which?

- **seasonal calendar**

(1) Discuss holidays in each month and the seasons.
(2) Ask such questions as, In which month is Thanksgiving celebrated? Help children turn to the correct month to answer each question.

Outdoor Play
See page 6.

Storytime
See page 7.

Indoor Play
See page 3 for suggested activities.

Art
Calendar Collage

- **calendars**
- **glue**
- **scissors**
- **construction paper**

Children can cut and glue pieces of calendar pages on paper to create a calendar collage.

Music
Play records. Children can pretend to be stiff, marching toy soldiers and then limp, wiggly rag dolls.

Snack
Frozen grapes taste great on a hot summer day!

Learning Time
Calendar Fun

- **calendar**
- **marking pen**

(1) Hold up calendar. Have children count how many months make up a year.
(2) Help children locate and circle their birthdays on calendar. Each child can tell the day of the week on which her or his birthday falls this year.
(3) Flip calendar pages to show each month as you slowly recite poem "A Pickle of a Year" and children repeat lines with you.

January, February—eat a pickle in the snow.
March and April—tie your pickle in a bow.
May, June, July—dip your pickle in a pie.
August and September—it's almost time to say bye-bye.
October and November—just one month left to go.
And that would be December—the year has gone, you know.

Outdoor Play
If weather permits, bring out a water table and water toys. Supervise water play closely.

Storytime
Make up a story about planning for a party on Saturday. Describe what you did each day of the week to plan for your party, starting on Sunday. If you wish, have the group participate in the storytelling.

September
Week 1

I bet I know how much 2 take away 1 is!

Numbers

Indoor Play
See page 3 for ideas.

Art
Number Book
- **crayons**
- **construction paper**
- **stapler**

(1) Each child can stack and fold 2–6 pieces of paper together.
(2) Staple each book on fold.
(3) Print title *My Number Book* on each child's book.
(4) Let children number each page in order and then draw 1 item on page 1, 2 items on page 2, and so on.

Music
Play different records. Children can play imaginary instruments to the music.

Snack
Serve cheese and crackers.

Learning Time
Drawing Numbers
- **large piece of paper**
- **crayons**

(1) Write numbers 1–5 on paper.
(2) Children can practice writing numbers while everyone sings "Numbers" (tune of "Mulberry Bush").
   Start up here and come straight down.
   Start up here and come straight down.
   Heigh-ho, what do you know!
   We made the number 1.
  Other verses:
   Half around, then straight across . . . (2)
   Half around, then half around . . . (3)
   Down, across, and then straight down . . . (4)
   Down, half around, and across at the top . . . (5)

Outdoor Play
Nice Baby
(1) Choose a child to be BABY.
(2) Others sit on ground. BABY crawls on all fours and says, "Wah, wah," to a player.
(3) That player pats BABY and says, "Nice baby," without smiling. BABY crawls to another player.
(4) First player to smile has to be next BABY.

Storytime
Tell and act out "Three Little Pigs."

Indoor Play

Have children count how many doors, windows, or other structures are in the room.

Art

Number Plates

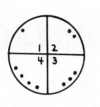

- paper plates
- marking pens
- seeds or beans
- glue

Help each child:

(1) divide plate into 4-8 wedges, using marking pen;
(2) number wedges and on each wedge, glue number of beans or seeds to correspond with number.

Music

Finger Plays

"Five Little Monkeys"   "Teasing Mr. Crocodile"

Circle Dances

"Farmer in the Dell"   "Ring around the Rosie"

Snack

Peanutty Balls

- 1 c. smooth peanut butter
- ½ c. honey
- ½ c. dry powdered milk
- nuts, raisins, granola, coconut, or carob chips (optional)

Children can mix ingredients and mold mixure into 1" balls.

Learning Time

Counting Beans

- marking pen
- egg carton
- beans or seeds

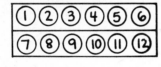

(1) Write numbers in egg carton compartments.
(2) Let children count out beans or seeds and place appropriate amount in each cup.

Outdoor Play

Bouncing Balls

Have children bounce 3 balls and sing "Bouncing Balls" (tune of "Mulberry Bush").

   Here's a ball, and here's a ball,
   And here's another one, you see.
   Shall we count them? Are you ready?
   One, two, three.

Storytime

See page 7.

Indoor Play

Calendar Games

Cut numbers from an old calendar. Have children find identical numbers and then have children put numbers in sequence.

Art

Number Cards

- marking pens or crayons
- 3" x 3" squares of construction paper

Help children write a number between 1 and 10 on each square. They can then color and draw on the cards.

Music

Everyone can sing this song (tune of "Mulberry Bush") and draw imaginary numbers in the air.

   Curve down and then around.
   Curve down and then around.
   Heigh-ho, what do you know!
   We made the number 6.
Other verses:
   Half across and then straight down . . . (7)
   Make an S and come back up . . . (8)
   Come around and then straight down . . . (9)
   Come straight down and then around . . . (10)

Snack

Fresh fruit with yogurt is yummy!

Learning Time

Number Scavenger Hunt

- number cards from art lesson
- 10 paper bags (flat-bottomed)
- marking pen

(1) Mark each bag with a different number from 1 to 10.
(2) Hide number cards.
(3) Let children find cards and sort them into bags.

Outdoor Play

Bag Bowling

- bags from Learning Time
- balls

(1) Set up empty bags.
(2) Have children take turns rolling balls toward bags.
(3) Everyone can call out numbers on bags as they're knocked down.

Storytime

See page 7.

September
Week 2

Nursery Rhymes

Indoor Play

Place small box on table. Children can practice shooting baskets with aluminum foil balls.

Art

Mary's Little Lamb

- **paper**
- **crayons**
- **cotton balls**
- **glue**

Help each child:
(1) draw a picture of a lamb;
(2) glue cotton balls on lamb for fur.

Music

Play lively music on record player. Have children pair up and create a dance to the music with their partners.

Snack/Learning Time

Curds and Whey

- **2 c. milk**
- **1 tbsp. vinegar**
- **salt**

(1) Heat milk and vinegar.
(2) Stir to separate curds and whey.
(3) Sprinkle with salt and refrigerate.
(4) Provide packaged banana chips and carrot chips for children to eat with their curds and whey.

Outdoor Play

Touch to Ten

Let children touch and count 10 objects that have something in common. All the objects might be smooth, rough, same color, or same shape.

Storytime

(1) Place stool or cushion in center of group.
(2) Select someone to play Miss Muffet and someone to play the spider. Let everyone have a turn.
(3) Have Miss Muffet sit on her "tuffet" (stool or cushion) and recite nursery rhyme "Little Miss Muffet."
(4) Spider should come at appropriate time, and Miss Muffet should run away.

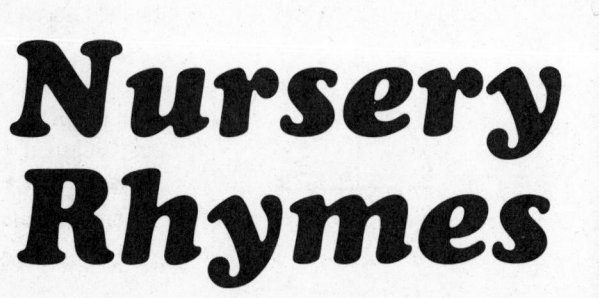

Indoor Play

Bring out dress-up clothes for children to wear.

Art

Sequence Nursery Rhymes

- **coloring books or old nursery rhyme books**
- **construction paper**
- **glue**
- **scissors**

Have each child:

(1) cut 3-5 pictures that illustrate a familiar nursery rhyme;
(2) glue each picture onto its own piece of paper.

Music

Nursery Rhymes

"Jack, Be Nimble"   "Humpty Dumpty"
"Jack and Jill"   "Baa, Baa, Black Sheep"

Circle Dances

"Looby Loo"   "Punchinello"
"Mulberry Bush"   "Skip to My Lou"

Snack

Serve "Humpty Dumpty" hard-boiled eggs with "Jack, Be Nimble" candlestick pretzel sticks. Provide juice to go with snack. Let children use crayons to draw faces on their eggs before cracking and peeling off shells.

Learning Time

Tell Me a Story

- **nursery rhyme pictures from art lesson**
- **flannel board (see page 7)**

(1) Mix up pictures and place them on flannel board.
(2) Have children put pictures back in sequence as you tell nursery rhyme.

Outdoor Play

Follow the Leader

(1) Let children take turns being leader.
(2) Others must copy leader's motions, such as jumping jacks, somersaults, hopping, skipping, touching toes, or stretching.

Storytime

(1) Bring out coloring books. You or the children can make up stories about the pictures.
(2) Let each child tell his or her impression of what Mother Goose looks like.

Indoor Play

Have nursery rhyme books available for children to look through.

Art

Spider

- **egg carton bottoms**
- **scissors**
- **marking pens**
- **pipe cleaners**

(1) Cut apart egg carton compartments. Give a section to each child.
(2) Children can draw a spider face on the section.
(3) They can then insert pipe cleaners for legs.

Music

Let children use the spiders from the art lesson as props while they sing "Itsy, Bitsy Spider."

Snack

How about sour cream and fresh peaches?

Learning Time

Refer to a children's encyclopedia or other illustrated resource. Tell the group about the body structure of spiders, about web spinning, and about how beneficial most common spiders are to the environment.

Outdoor Play

Children can play hopscotch.

Storytime

(1) Let children tell and act out various nursery rhymes of their choice.
(2) Tell a personalized story about the children: For example: "Once upon a time there were ____ children. Their names were ____ , ____ , (and so on). They came to school one day, and this is what they did."

September
Week 3

Fall

Indoor Play
Have several pairs of socks available in different colors and sizes. Let children mix and match them.

Learning Time
Fall Walk
(1) Discuss signs of fall.
(2) Everyone can take a walk and look for colorful leaves, pinecones, pine needles, cocoons, and other signs of autumn.
(3) Collect in paper bags any "treasures"—twigs, stones, fallen leaves—found along the way.

Music
See page 5.

Snack
Cut up apples.

Art
Fall Collages
- paper plates
- treasures from fall walk
- glue
- marking pen

(1) Help children print *Fall* on plates.
(2) Children can glue fall treasures on paper plates.

Outdoor Play
Painting with Grass
- long grass
- water in bucket

Children can:
(1) dip long grass into bucket of water;
(2) use grass like a brush and paint on cement.

Storytime
Opposite Game
(1) Say a word and have child say a word that means the opposite. For example: stop—go, under—over, up—down, in—out, hot—cold, happy—sad, no—yes, sick—well.
(2) Tell a story about a little boy who always did the opposite of what he was told. For example: "If his mother told him to wash his face, he would get it dirty. If his father told him to speak quietly, he would speak loudly."

Indoor Play

Let the group help make playhouses by covering tables with sheets. Encourage imaginative play.

Art

Leaf Impressions

- crayons
- lightweight paper
- paper clips
- fall leaves

Help each child:
(1) place leaves between 2 sheets of paper;
(2) clip the sheets together;
(3) rub crayon over entire surface and see leaf impressions appear "like magic."

Music

Finger Plays and Songs

"Open, Shut Them"   "I'm a Little Teapot"
"Wheels on the Bus"   "Happy and You Know It"
"Where Is Thumbkin?"   "Teddy Bear"

Circle Dances

"Hokey Pokey"   "Ring around the Rosie"

Snack/Learning Time

Yummy No-Bake Cookies

- 2 c. sugar
- ½ c. milk
- ¼ lb. butter
- 5 tbsp. cocoa
- 2½ c. quick oats
- 1 tsp. vanilla

(1) Let children mix first 4 ingredients.
(2) Boil mixture for 1½ minutes.
(3) Remove from heat and add vanilla and oats.
(4) Beat until stiff.
(5) Let children drop mixture by spoonfuls onto waxed paper.
(6) Let cookies cool.

Outdoor Play

Balloon Kite

- inflated balloons
- marking pens
- string

(1) Have children gently draw faces or designs on balloons.
(2) Help children attach strings to balloons.
(3) Have them run with balloons, letting balloons "fly."

Storytime

See page 7.

Indoor Play

See page 3.

Art

Fall Tree

- construction paper in fall colors
- marking pens
- glue

Have each child:
(1) draw a tree trunk and branches on a piece of construction paper;
(2) tear small leaf shapes from various colors of paper;
(3) glue leaves on tree;
(4) glue some leaves at bottom of paper to show that autumn leaves are falling off tree.

Music

Let children take turns tumbling and practicing cartwheels to music.

Snack

Serve granola and carob chips with milk.

Learning Time

Fall Poem

- red, yellow, and brown leaves

(1) Hold up appropriate color leaves while everyone says this fall poem.
    One, two, three pretty leaves I see.
    One is red, one is yellow.
    One is brown—a funny fellow.
    One, two, three pretty leaves I see.
(2) Each child can pretend to be a leaf blowing in the wind and floating slowly to the ground.

Outdoor Play

Jumping through Leaves
Children can:
(1) take turns raking leaves outside;
(2) huddle down in pile of leaves;
(3) count to 3 out loud and then jump up;
(4) walk and run in leaves to make crackling sound.

Storytime

Read or tell the story of Cinderella.

September

Week 4

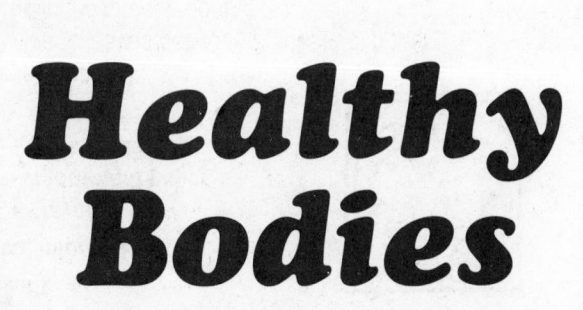

Hey, I found the Band-Aids!

Healthy Bodies

Indoor Play
Bring out aluminum foil. Have the children create sculptures.

Art
Fingerprint Designs
- **construction paper**
- **paper towels moistened in ink (recipe on page 85)**
- **crayons**

Let each child:
(1) press finger on inky paper towel;
(2) gently press finger on construction paper;
(3) make crayon drawings around dry fingerprint.

Music
Songs
"Growing" (tune of "Are You Sleeping?")
   We need food, and we need water.
   We need sleep, lots of sleep,
   To make our bodies grow
   From our heads down to our toes.
   Grow, grow, grow,
   Grow, grow, grow.
"Bingo"   "Happy and You Know It"

Snack
Reinforce good nutrition with fresh fruits or vegetables.

Learning Time
Staying Healthy
(1) Discuss what we need to stay healthy and grow: food, water, sleep, exercise, fresh air.
(2) Discuss how it feels to be sick, mentioning headache, stomachache, fever, sore throat.
(3) Discuss what we do when we're sick: go to bed, go to the doctor, drink liquids, take medicine.

Outdoor Play
Simon Says
Play the part of Simon, giving commands for the children to follow. If you give a command without first saying "Simon says," children don't have to follow the command.

Storytime
What If? Story
Begin a story: "What if it started to snow in my bedroom?" Let children take turns telling rest of story.

Indoor Play

See page 3.

Art

Body Parts

- construction paper
- scissors
- brass fasteners
- yarn
- crayons
- glue

Help children:

(1) cut out ovals and circles for body parts;
(2) attach fasteners at body joints;
(3) glue yarn on for hair;
(4) draw features with crayons.

Music

Finger Plays and Songs

Everyone can sing and act out "Healthy Bodies" (tune of "Row Your Boat"). Repeat the verse 3 times, each time more quickly. While singing, everyone points to parts of body and then stretches arms above head on last line.

Head, arms, fingers, hands,
Shoulders, knees, and toes,
Eyes, ears, nose, and mouth,
A healthy body grows.

Circle Dances

"Looby Loo"   "Mulberry Bush"

Snack

Serve apples today "to keep the doctor away."

Learning Time

Healthy Heart

(1) Discuss heart as a pump and how it pushes blood through our bodies. The more we exercise, the faster it pushes blood through our bodies.
(2) Help children find their pulse.
(3) Have children do jumping jacks or run around and then find pulse again and notice how beat has gotten faster.
(4) Let each child press ear against someone else's chest and listen to heartbeat.

Outdoor Play

Supervise group in a tug of war on a roomy, grassy area.

Storytime

Let the group share experiences at doctors' and dentists' offices.

Field Trip

Visit to a Medical Office

Call ahead for permission. This is an opportunity for children to visit the office of a doctor, dentist, or optometrist without feeling anxiety or apprehension. If possible, have a doctor or a nurse speak briefly with the children.

Indoor Play

What's Missing?

- items from toy doctor kits
- tray

(1) Place several items on tray.
(2) While children cover eyes, remove an item.
(3) Have children guess which item is missing.

Music

Have children sing "Growing" (tune of "Are You Sleeping?") on page 74 and "Healthy Bodies" (tune of "Row Your Boat") shown on this page.

Learning Time

Doctor's Office

- Popsicle sticks (or real tongue depressors)
- cotton balls
- bandages
- dolls (optional)
- toy doctor kit (optional)
- white shirts (adult size)

Have children take turns being doctor, nurse, and patient. Nurses and doctors can wear white shirts. Show children how to bandage ankles and wrists.

October

Week 1

Teacher, when you were a little girl, how many dinosaurs lived on your block?

Dinosaurs

Field Trip

Visit to Library or Museum

Visit the library and check out books that have pictures and information about dinosaurs. If your local museum has displays of dinosaur skeletons or dioramas of prehistoric scenes, take your field trip to the museum.

Snack

Walking Treat

- **apples**
- **peanut butter or cheese**

(1) Children can wash and dry apples.
(2) Core the apples for the children.
(3) Children can fill apples with peanut butter or cheese.
(4) Take snack on field trip.

Art

Dinosaur Shadow Box

- **shoe boxes**
- **crayons**
- **grass (real or synthetic)**
- **toy dinosaurs or playdough dinosaurs that children make**
- **rocks**

Help each child:
(1) draw mountains or marsh on inside bottom of shoe box;
(2) turn box on side and fill shadow box floor with grass, rocks, and dinosaurs.

Outdoor Play

Dinosaur Is Sleeping

One child is DINOSAUR who pretends to be asleep while everyone else hides. Then everyone yells "Wake up, dinosaur." DINOSAUR wakes up and tries to find everyone. Let children take turns being DINOSAUR.

Storytime

Have the children tell stories, using their dinosaur shadow boxes as props.

Indoor Play
Children can stomp around, pretending to be dinosaurs.

Art
Modeling Goop Dinosaurs
- **Modeling goop (recipe on page 4)**

Let children mold goop into mountains, trees, dinosaurs, and other prehistoric things. You may wish to provide posters or picture books of dinosaurs as samples.

Music
Finger Plays and Songs
"Hiding Dinosaurs"
   Dinosaur, dinosaur,
   Where can you be?
   Hiding behind me (*hands behind back*)
   Where you cannot see.
   Now you see one. (*bring out one hand*)
   It's been waiting for you.
   Here comes another, (*bring out other hand*)
   And now you see two.
"Jack-in-the-Box"   "Twinkle, Twinkle"
"Five in the Bed"   "Yankee Doodle"

Snack
Coconut Shake
- **2 c. plain yogurt**
- **½ c. shredded coconut**
- **4 c. pineapple juice**

Mix ingredients. Shake them in closed container or use blender.

Learning Time
All about Dinosaurs
(1) Use reference books to aid discussion of dinosaurs. Talk about how big dinosaurs were, what they ate, how they moved around, and so on.
(2) Make statements to which children answer yes or no. Use such statements about dinosaurs as:
   Dinosaurs ate bushes. (YES)
   Dinosaurs drove cars. (NO)
   Some dinosaurs could fly. (YES)
   Dinosaurs lived in houses. (NO)

Outdoor Play
See page 6.

Storytime
See page 7.

Indoor Play
See page 3.

Art
Dinosaur Sock Puppets
- **old socks**
- **cloth scraps**
- **felt**
- **cardboard**
- **glue**
- **scissors**

(1) Have each child stuff toe of sock with scraps.
(2) Cut pieces of cardboard shaped as shown. Then have children fold them in half and glue them onto insteps of socks.
(3) Children can then glue on eyes cut out of felt.

Music
Children can play with their sock puppets while singing "Dinosaurs" (tune of "Row Your Boat").
   Dinosaurs, dinosaurs
   Eating fruits and weeds
   Take a bite and chew it well
   And then spit out the seeds.

Snack
See page 5.

Learning Time
Have children look through picture books of dinosaurs.

Outdoor Play
See Dinosaur Is Sleeping game on page 76.

Storytime
Good Friend Jake
- **flannel board (see page 7)**
- **paper cutouts of 4 dinosaurs, blue sock, red and blue beads, weeds, rock, tree**

Place dinosaurs on flannel board and add other props as you tell this rhyming story: "Three baby dinosaurs were playing by a tree when they heard a voice say, 'You can't catch me.' The first baby dinosaur looked behind a rock, but all she could find was a big blue sock. The second baby dinosaur looked between some weeds, but all he could find were some blue and red beads. The third baby dinosaur looked up in the tree and yelled, 'I can see you. Can you see me?' All of a sudden, the tree began to shake, and out of the tree fell their good friend Jake."

October
Week 2

How come tuna fish can't taste like chocolate cake?

My Five Senses

Indoor Play
Bring out assorted shoes and let children practice tying, lacing, and buckling.

Art
Object Puzzle

- **various objects or shapes for tracing**
- **construction paper**
- **crayons**

Have the children:
(1) trace the outline of objects on paper;
(2) mix up the objects;
(3) match each object to its outline.

Music
Rubber Band Guitars

- **cardboard boxes without lids**
- **rubber bands**

Help each child:
(1) wrap rubber bands of various sizes around open box;
(2) strum fingers over rubber bands while singing.

Snack
Let the group sample foods that are sweet, salty, sour, and bitter.

Learning Time
Senses Walk

Take a walk with the group. Encourage them to use all 5 senses. Take a snack along for sense of taste.

Outdoor Play
Who's Got the Button?

- **button**

Choose an IT and a BUTTON PASSER. Others stand in circle facing each other with hands behind backs. IT stands in center. BUTTON PASSER walks around outside of circle, pretending to put button in each player's hand but actually putting it in hand of only 1 player. BUTTON PASSER then says to IT, "Button, button, who's got the button?" IT guesses. The child with the button becomes new BUTTON PASSER. Old BUTTON PASSER becomes next IT.

Storytime
What If? Story

Begin a story: "What if your pet started to talk to you?" Let children take turns responding.

Indoor Play

See page 3.

Art

Smell Plates

- paper plates
- assorted "smelly" items, such as cloves, bay leaves, mint, other leafy spices, perfumed cotton
- marking pen
- glue

(1) Help each child print title *My Smell Plate*.
(2) They can arrange and glue smelly objects on plate.

Music

Finger Plays

Have everyone follow words to the poem "Listening."
   Let your hands go clap, clap, clap.
   Let your fingers snap, snap, snap.
   Let your lips go very round,
   But do not make a sound. Shhhh!
"Open, Shut Them"   "Five Little Monkeys"

Snack

Frozen Yogurt

- 8 oz. fruit cocktail
- 12 oz. plain yogurt
- ½ banana
- Popsicle sticks
- paper cups

(1) Mix first 3 ingredients in blender.
(2) Pour into small paper cups and have children insert Popsicle sticks. Freeze mixture until ready to eat.

Learning Time

Guessing Smells

- blindfold
- assorted "smelly" foods, such as pickles, bologna, tuna, onion

Blindfold a child. Let child smell 1 item and try to guess what it is. Keep foods hidden.

Outdoor Play

See page 6.

Storytime

Which Sense Am I?

Give clues and have children guess which sense is being used. For example:
   telephone ringing (hearing)
   licking a lollipop (taste)
   finger painting (touch)

Indoor Play

Matching Pairs

- pairs of assorted small objects, such as buttons, cotton balls, erasers, beans
- egg carton

(1) Scatter all objects on table.
(2) Have children place 1 object in each egg carton compartment so paired objects are side by side.

Art

Tying Shoes

- cardboard
- shoelaces
- crayons
- scissors
- hole punch

(1) Help each child trace shoe on cardboard and cut it out.
(2) Punch 3 sets of holes on each cardboard shoe.
(3) Children can practice tying and lacing cardboard shoes.

Music

Nursery Rhymes

"Little Miss Muffett"   "Mary Had a Little Lamb"
"Jack, Be Nimble"   "I'm a Little Teapot"

Snack

Make popcorn and have children watch, listen, taste, touch, and smell.

Learning Time

Listen

- container with lid
- objects from Indoor Play
- blindfold

(1) Blindfold a child.
(2) Place 1 object in container and put on lid.
(3) Have blindfolded child shake jar and, by listening, identify object in jar.

Outdoor Play

See page 6.

Storytime

Read or tell the story "Jack and the Beanstalk."

October
Week 3

Please, can I have one? I'll be your best friend!

In the Country

Indoor Play
See page 3.

Art
Homemade Finger Paint
- shelf paper
- ½ c. liquid nontoxic paint
- 1 tsp. liquid detergent
- 1 tsp. liquid starch
- newspapers or plastic tablecloth
- aprons

(1) Everyone should wear aprons. Cover working surface well.
(2) Mix paint, detergent, and starch.
(3) Spoon a small amount on center of paper. Using their fingers, children slowly spread paint out to edges of paper to create designs.

Music
Nursery Rhymes and Songs

"Jack and Jill"   "Twinkle, Twinkle"
"Humpty Dumpty"   "Yankee Doodle"
"Baa, Baa, Black Sheep"   "Row Your Boat"

Circle Dances

"Looby Loo"   "Hokey Pokey"

Snack/Learning Time
A Pretend Hike
- picnic lunch or snack
- blanket

(1) Have children hike through play area, pretending they are outdoors. Suggest that they pretend to be climbing up a mountain, walking through a stream, crawling through bushes, discovering a beautiful spot for a picnic.
(2) Spread blanket and enjoy snack or picnic lunch.

Outdoor Play
Take photographs of the children at play.

Storytime
Sharing Stories
Children can share a story about a favorite outing—camping, hiking, going to the beach, or some other outdoor experience.

Indoor Play

What's Missing?

- basket
- assorted country items, such as wheat sheaf, old coffee pot, calico napkin, apple

(1) Place 5 or 6 items in basket. Let a child remove an item while others cover their eyes.
(2) Others try to guess which item is missing. Child who guesses gets to remove item next.

Art

Country Character Puppets

- paper plates
- stapler
- scissors
- crayons

(1) Help each child cut a plate in half and staple to another plate, leaving opening for hand.
(2) They can then draw faces to make country characters—farmers, loggers, ranchers, or animals from the country.

Music

The group can sing songs or listen to music while playing with puppets.

Snack/Learning Time

Haystacks

- butterscotch bits
- 1 can chow mein noodles
- 1 c. peanuts (optional)
- waxed paper
- saucepan

(1) Melt butterscotch bits in pan.
(2) Stir in peanuts and noodles.
(3) Drop a teaspoonful at a time onto waxed paper.
(4) Cool haystacks.

Outdoor Play

Cornmeal Play

- cornmeal (in pans)
- plastic spoons
- plastic bowls
- measuring cups
- pitchers
- funnels

Take everything outdoors so group can enjoy playing with cornmeal.

Storytime

Choose a book about living in the country. Before reading the book, point out the author's and illustrator's names. Explain what they do.

Field Trip

A Visit to the Country
Possible trips include:
    berry picking
    state fair
    apple picking
    hiking
    nature trail
If you conduct the art lesson first, children can take their "binoculars" on the field trip.

Art

Binoculars

- toilet paper rolls (2 for each child)
- yarn
- scissors
- crayons
- tape

Help each child:
(1) tape 2 rolls together;
(2) attach yarn to make a shoulder strap;
(3) decorate binoculars with crayon designs.

Learning Time

Straw Blowing

- straws
- paint
- construction paper

Have each child:
(1) put several drops of paint on paper;
(2) blow through straw to spread paint;
(3) let colors run together and discover how to blend colors.

Storytime

Have each child name a color from the straw-blowing paintings and mention something of that color in the country. For example, if the child names green, he or she might mention trees.

October

Week 4

Nah....I think I changed my mind. I'd rather be a witch.

Halloween

Indoor Play
See page 3.

Art
Stuffed Pumpkins

- small paper bags
- newspaper
- masking tape
- orange poster paint
- paintbrushes
- black construction paper
- scissors

Help each child:

(1) stuff paper bag with crumpled newspaper;
(2) twist bag shut and wrap tape around twisted end to make a 3″ stem;
(3) paint the stuffed pumpkin;
(4) cut facial features out of construction paper and stick them on pumpkin before paint dries.

Music
See page 5.

Snack
Biscuit Ghosts

- refrigerator biscuits
- cinnamon and sugar mixture
- butter

(1) Let the children separate biscuits and shape each like a ghost.
(2) They can roll biscuits in butter and then in cinnamon and sugar mixture.
(3) Bake biscuits as directed on package.

Learning Time
How to Trick-or-Treat

- various masks
- treats
- paper bags

(1) Let children demonstrate how a person changes in appearance when he or she puts on a mask.
(2) Discuss traditional trick-or-treating.
(3) Have children pretend to trick-or-treat. Let a child answer the door and pass out treats to trick-or-treaters.

Outdoor Play
Follow the Leader

See directions for game on page 35. As a variation, have leader give 2 or 3 simple commands for group to follow. Leader might say, for example, "Go to the door, knock three times, and turn around."

Storytime
Read a Halloween story.

Indoor Play

Have some costumes available for dress-up fun.

Art

Torn Black Cats

- crayons
- black construction paper

Help each child:

(1) fold paper in half lengthwise;

(2) hold paper on folded side and tear a half circle from open edges, as shown;

(3) from half circle, tear a cat-shaped head;

(4) color a face on cat;

(5) insert head into body by cutting slit on fold.

Music

Finger Plays

"Three Little Witches" (tune of "Ten Little Indians")
    One little, two little, three little witches
    Flying over haystacks, flying over ditches,
    Sliding down moonbeams without any hitches.
    Heigh-ho, Halloween's here.

"Teasing Mr. Crocodile"   "Five Little Monkeys"

Snack

Black Cat Cupcakes

- **chocolate-frosted cupcakes**
- **small green candies**
- **black licorice (cut into small strips)**

Have each child:

(1) place green candies on cupcake for eyes and nose;

(2) use licorice strips for whiskers, ears, and mouth.

Learning Time

A Knock on the Door

Begin the story by making a knocking sound and saying, "Who's knocking at my door?" Each child takes a turn describing who could be behind the door and what the visitor wants.

Outdoor Play

Goblin, Goblin, Ghost

Follow rules to Duck, Duck, Goose on page 11.

Storytime

See page 7.

Field Trip

A Visit to a Pumpkin Patch

Buy a pumpkin to be used later for carving and making pumpkin seeds.

Learning Time

Pin the Nose on the Pumpkin

- **pumpkin**
- **construction paper**
- **scissors**
- **tape**
- **blindfold**

(1) Draw eyes and mouth on pumpkin.

(2) Cut out several nose shapes from paper.

(3) Blindfold child and have that child stand a few feet away from pumpkin.

(4) Child tries to tape nose in correct space on pumpkin's face.

(5) Have children take turns.

Art

Carve the pumpkin purchased at the pumpkin patch.

Snack

Roasted Pumpkin Seeds

- **2 c. dried pumpkin seeds**
- **2 tbsp. melted butter**
- **½ tsp. Worcestershire sauce**
- **salt**

The group can help:

(1) mix first 3 ingredients;

(2) spread seeds on cookie sheet;

(3) sprinkle seeds with salt.

Bake seeds at 350° until golden brown.

November
Week 1

BARBER SHOP

Hey, mister, when he's finished, can I have a ride on that chair?

Community Workers

Field Trip
Visit to a Barber or Hairdresser
Arrange for a visit at a time when the group can watch the barber or hairdresser at work. Discuss the equipment used.

Art
Fringed Haircut
- construction paper
- scissors
- crayons

Help each child:
(1) cut large circle from paper;
(2) draw eyes, nose, mouth, and ears on circle;
(3) make small cuts (fringe) around circle to create hair.

Learning Time
Barber Play
- white aprons
- towels
- combs
- table and chairs

(1) Let children take turns being barber and customer.
(2) The barber can pretend to cut hair, using scissor motion with fingers.

Storytime
How about telling the story of Rapunzel?

Indoor Play

Bring out dress-up clothes and be sure to include all the hats you can find. Try to find baseball caps, cowboy hats, hard hats, fire fighter hats, and hats appropriate for business people.

Art

Horizontal Puzzles

- **construction paper**
- **magazines**
- **scissors**

Help each child:
(1) find a picture of a community worker in a magazine;
(2) glue picture on paper;
(3) cut into 3 horizontal strips;
(4) mix up pieces and put them back in order.
Children can share puzzles.

Music

Use marching sticks (wooden spoons or Lincoln Logs) to tap to music.

Snack

Try dried fruit for a change of pace.

Learning Time

Mail Carrier Fun

- **large bag**
- **index cards**
- **marking pen**
- **large envelopes**

(1) Write each child's name on several index cards. Put cards into large bag.
(2) Give each child an envelope with his or her name on it.
(3) Choose a child to pose as a mail carrier picking cards out of bag and delivering them into appropriate envelopes. Let younger children match pictures instead of names.

Outdoor Play

Bring out big boxes to use as props in an imaginary play.

Storytime

Tell a continuous story about a letter that is swept up by the wind and lands in different situations. The letter could land on a fast-moving train, in a bear's cage, or in a sprinkler.

Field Trip

Visit to a Post Office

(1) Before going on trip, write short notes or let group help you draw pictures to send to special people. Have children observe as you place notes or pictures in envelopes and address envelopes.
(2) Buy stamps at the post office and show children how to moisten a stamp, place it on a letter, and drop letter in mailbox. Have enough pieces of correspondence so that each child can mail a letter.

Art

Post Office Ink

- **1 tsp. food coloring**
- **3 tbsp. liquid starch**
- **1 tbsp. water**

Let children mix ingredients to make ink for rubber stamps.

Learning Time

Play Post Office

- **paper towels moistened with ink from art lesson**
- **rubber stamps**
- **box with slit**
- **junk mail**

(1) Children can set up a post office and use the box as a mailbox.
(2) Let children take turns delivering mail.

November

Week 2

When Fluffy's five, she's gonna be as big as us.

Shapes and Sizes

Indoor Play
Bring out blocks for the children to build imaginary structures.

Art
Shape Me Cards
- **scissors**
- **crayons**
- **construction paper**

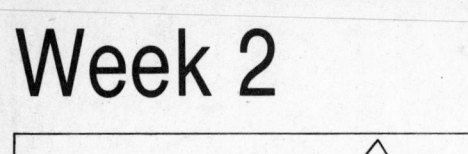

Help each child:
(1) fold piece of paper in half to resemble a card;
(2) unfold card and cut geometric shape from middle of card cover;
(3) close card and trace shape onto inner page;
(4) open card and draw a picture around the traced shape.

Music
Finger Plays
"Make a Circle"
  Make a circle, make a square,
  Put your fingers in the air.
  Make a rectangle, make a triangle,
  Let your fingers jingle jangle.
"Where Is Thumbkin?"   "Five in the Bed"

Circle Dances
"Teddy Bear"   "Farmer in the Dell"

Snack
Fill celery sticks with cream cheese or egg salad.

Learning Time
Shape Me Rhyme
- **Shape Me cards from art lesson**

Hold up 1 card at a time and have group recite poem below, changing first 2 words according to shape on card.
  Circle, circle, what can you be? (*card closed*)
  Open the card and you will see. (*open card*)

Outdoor Play
Have children take crayons and tablets outdoors and look for interesting shapes to sketch.

Storytime
Tell the story of the Ugly Duckling.

Indoor Play
Have children try making shapes with their fingers or bodies.

Art
Sandpaper Shapes

- **crayons**
- **sandpaper**
- **scissors**

Have children:
(1) draw shapes on sandpaper;
(2) color inside the shapes;
(3) cut out shapes.

Music
Children can stretch and exercise to records.

Snack
Cinnamon Toast Triangles

- **cinnamon and sugar mixture**
- **butter**
- **bread**

Let the children help prepare this snack.
(1) Toast bread.
(2) Butter toast and top with cinnamon and sugar mixture.
(3) Cut toast into 2 or 4 triangles.

Learning Time
Sandpaper Shape Game

- **masking tape**
- **sandpaper shapes from art lesson**
- **blindfold**

(1) Tape shapes on wall or flannel board.
(2) Blindfold a child.
(3) The child feels a shape and tries to identify it.

Outdoor Play
Newspaper Ball

- **newspaper**
- **tape**

(1) Children choose partners.
(2) Each pair makes a ball by crumpling newspaper into desired size.
(3) Children can kick or volley the ball or play baseball, using an empty paper towel roll as a bat.

Storytime
Read or tell the story "The Princess and the Pea."

Indoor Play
See page 3.

Art
Shape Mobiles

- **yarn (different lengths)**
- **construction paper**
- **scissors**
- **wooden hangers**
- **foil**
- **stapler**

Help each child:
(1) wrap hanger with foil;
(2) cut shapes from construction paper;
(3) tie yarn on hanger;
(4) staple shapes onto ends of yarn.

Music
Circle Rhythm Game
(1) Use tape or chalk to make a circle on the floor.
(2) Have children clap different rhythms. They can clap even rhythms for walking or running and uneven rhythms for skipping or galloping.
(3) Children move to the rhythm around the circle.

Snack/Learning Time
Creating Shapes to Eat

- **slices of cheese**
- **raisins**
- **stick pretzels**
- **Cheerios**

(1) Have children make triangles with slices of cheese.
(2) They can make squares and rectangles with pretzels.
(3) Cheerios and raisins can serve as circles.

Outdoor Play
See page 6.

Storytime
Choose a story that no one knows. Stop reading occasionally and have a child predict what will happen next.

November

Week 3

Isn't grass a green vegetable?

Fruits and Vegetables

Indoor Play
See page 3.

Art
Sculptured Fruit

- construction paper
- tape
- scissors
- newspaper
- paint
- paintbrushes

(1) Help each child cut out 2 identical fruit shapes.
(2) Place each pair of shapes together and tape most of the way around the outer edge.
(3) Have the children crumple up small pieces of newspaper and stuff fruit.
(4) Tape the sculptures closed.
(5) Children can paint their scupltures.

Music
Play the radio and have children dance to different types of music. Change stations for variety.

Snack
How about fruit salad?

Learning Time
What's Produce?

- fruits and vegetables

(1) Name and show each fruit and vegetable.
(2) Explain that we eat different parts of plants. Hold up examples and explain that we eat:
    seeds (corn and wheat)
    flowers (broccoli and cauliflower)
    stems (celery)
    roots (potatoes and onions)
    leaves (lettuce and spinach)
(3) Give each child a fruit or vegetable. Call out a command. Child holding the produce named follows command. For example:
    Tomato, turn around.
    Lettuce, jump up and down.
    Orange, clap hands.

Outdoor Play
The group might want to continue playing the fruit and vegetable game outdoors. Let each child have a chance to give commands.

Storytime
See page 7.

Indoor Play

Children can have lots of fun playing with partially inflated balloons.

Art

Fruit and Vegetable Stamps

- **construction paper**
- **assorted produce, such as potatoes and apples**
- **shallow bowls**
- **knife**
- **paint**

(1) Cut produce in half or into manageable pieces.
(2) Pour small amount of paint into bowls.
(3) Let each child dip cut edge of produce into paint and stamp it on paper. Encourage them to try various stamps.

Music

Finger Plays and Songs

"Five Little Monkeys"   "Teddy Bear"
"Wheels on the Bus"   "This Old Man"

Circle Dances

"London Bridge"   "Farmer in the Dell"

Snack

Raisin Carrot Salad

- **½ c. raisins**
- **1 carrot**
- **mayonnaise**
- **cottage cheese or crackers**

Let the group help:
(1) grate carrots and add raisins;
(2) moisten salad with mayonnaise;
(3) serve with cottage cheese or crackers.

Learning Time

Grocery Store Play

- **play money**
- **toy food cans and boxes**
- **paper bags**
- **wallet**
- **toy cash register or egg carton**

Have the group:
(1) display toy food cans and boxes;
(2) place some money in wallet and some in register;
(3) choose roles for cashier and customers;
(4) use bags to carry groceries.

Outdoor Play

See page 6.

Storytime

See page 7.

Field Trip

Visit to the Grocery

(1) With your group, walk or drive to a local store.
(2) Discuss which kind of produce are fruits and which are vegetables.
(3) Buy several produce samples to taste later.

Art

Vegetable and Fruit Mural

- **shelf or butcher paper**
- **crayons or marking pens**

Have the group draw fruit bins or boxes on paper as shown, and then have them draw different fruits and vegetables inside bins.

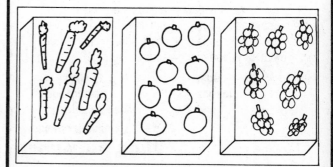

Snack/Learning Time

Tasting Produce

- **fruits and vegetables**

Have the children examine and taste various fruits and vegetables, noticing color, size, shape, seeds, skin or covering, and taste.

November

Week 4

> Why are all turkeys named Tom?

Thanksgiving

Indoor Play

See page 3.

Art

"Bead" Necklaces

- Cheerios
- shoelaces
- straws (cut into 1" pieces)
- macaroni (uncooked)

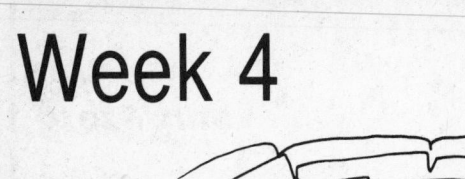

Have each child:

(1) tie knot at 1 end of shoelace;
(2) string Cheerios, macaroni, and straws;
(3) knot other end of shoelace and tie ends together.

Music

Lead the children in stretching and jogging to music.

Snack

Indian Hoe Cake

- 1 c. cornmeal
- ¾ c. boiling water
- 1 tsp. salt
- 3 tbsp. butter

(1) Butter a cookie sheet that has sides and place it in refrigerator for 15 minutes.
(2) Let children help mix ingredients.
(3) Pour batter into cookie sheet, spreading evenly.
(4) Bake at 300° for 45 minutes or until light brown.

Learning Time

Feathered Numbers

- construction paper
- flannel board (see page 7)
- pen
- scissors
- tape

(1) Cut out 10 feather shapes from paper. Mark them 1-10 and put loop of tape on back of each.
(2) Have group sing "Ten Little Indians." Place feathers on board as numbers are mentioned in song.
(3) Remove feathers as group counts backward in second verse.
(4) Hand out feathers. Children stand up as numbers they are holding are mentioned during first verse and sit down as they are mentioned in second verse.

Outdoor Play

Choose a child to be HUNTER and other children to be TURKEYS in a game of tag.

Storytime

The group can exchange stories about how they celebrate Thanksgiving.

Indoor Play

See page 3.

Art

Indian and Colonial Hats

- construction paper in assorted colors
- glue
- yarn
- stapler
- scissors

Have each child cut and assemble hat of his or her choice. Supervise the stapling or do this step for the children.

Indian Hat:

(1) Cut a band to fit around head and staple closed.
(2) Cut out several feather shapes and fringe edges.
(3) Staple feathers to band.

Colonial Hat:

(1) Cut a large piece of black paper as shown.
(2) Staple together corners 1 and 2 and corners 3 and 4, as shown.
(3) Cut out a buckle shape to glue on hat.
(4) Staple on yarn ties.

Music

See page 5.

Snack/Learning Time

Thanksgiving Feast

- table
- hats from art lesson
- a nutritious snack

(1) Discuss the first Thanksgiving and how the settlers and Indians cooperated to make a big feast.
(2) Let children help set table with today's snack.
(3) Have children wear hats they made.
(4) Have each child state a couple of things for which he or she is thankful.

Outdoor Play

Jump on the Blanket

(1) Place an old blanket on the ground.
(2) Children stand around edge of blanket.
(3) Call out, "Everyone jump on the blanket" or "Everyone jump off the blanket."
(4) If you don't say "everyone," children should not jump.

Storytime

Read or tell the story of Henny Penny.

Indoor Play

Let children play with stuffed animals and puppets.

Art

Turkey Handprint

- construction paper
- crayons

Have each child:

(1) trace hand on paper;
(2) color the thumb red and each finger a different color;
(3) color the palm to make the turkey's body and draw features.

Music

Songs

"Little Turkey" (tune of "I'm a Little Teapot")
  I'm a little turkey, my name is Ted.
  Here are my feathers, and here is my head.
  Gobble, gobble, gobble is what I say.
  Quick! Run! It's Thanksgiving Day.

"Teddy Bear"   "Pop! Goes the Weasel"

Circle Dances

"Farmer in the Dell"   "Ring around the Rosie"

Snack/Learning Time

Gobble-up Peanut Butter Sandwiches

- bread
- peanut butter
- carrot sticks
- celery sticks
- green olives with pimiento

(1) Help children spread peanut butter on bread.
(2) Let them arrange sandwiches on plates as shown, with carrot stick as turkey neck, olive as head, and celery sticks as feathers.
(3) Then the children can gobble up their sandwiches!

Outdoor Play

Lead the group in a game of Simon Says that uses position commands, such as:
  jump on the sidewalk
  run around in a big circle
  stand beside your best friend
  hold your hands above your head
Then let the children take turns being Simon.

Storytime

Read or tell the story "The Fisherman and His Wife."

December

Week 1

If I promise to walk and feed him every day, can I take him back to school?

Zoo Animals

Indoor Play

Cover table with large blanket. Tell the group to pretend they are camping in the jungle.

Art

Molding Animals

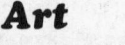

- **refrigerator cookie dough**
- **cookie sheets**

(1) Let the children flatten and mold dough into animal shapes and place shapes directly onto cookie sheets.

(2) Bake cookies as directed on the package.

Music

Finger Plays and Songs

"Teasing Mr. Crocodile"   "Bingo"

"Where Is Thumbkin?"   "Jack-in-the-Box"

Circle Dance

Everyone can make appropriate animal movements while singing "Animal Walk" (tune of "Mulberry Bush").

Look what the elephants can do in the zoo,

Can do in the zoo, can do in the zoo.

Look what the elephants can do in the zoo,

And you can do it, too.

Repeat the song, naming different animals.

Snack

Serve animal cookies from art lesson with milk.

Learning Time

Making Up Riddles

Using these examples, make up your own riddles with the group.

I have no legs. I rhyme with lake.

Who am I? (a snake)

I am brown and fuzzy. I rhyme with care.

Who am I? (a bear)

I love to swing. I rhyme with spunky.

Who am I? (a monkey)

Outdoor Play

See page 6.

Storytime

What If? Story

Children can take turns telling stories that answer the question, What if a giraffe followed you home from the zoo?

Indoor Play
See page 3.

Art
Animal Finger Puppets

- **construction paper**
- **scissors**
- **crayons or marking pens**

(1) Cut out animal shapes as shown.
(2) Cut out circles for fingers.
(3) Let children add features and insert fingers in holes.

Music
Children take turns showing how an elephant would sound and look if it sang and danced to music.

Snack/Learning Time
Zoo Sandwiches

- **bread**
- **cheese slices**
- **raisins**
- **animal cookie cutters**

Have each child:
(1) cut a cheese slice with cookie cutter;
(2) place cheese on slice of bread;
(3) add raisins for features, such as eyes, tail, nose, and ears.

Outdoor Play
Animal Movements

(1) Choose a child to be leader.
(2) Others will follow the leader making various animal movements. Suggest that they slither, scamper, gallop, climb, swing, and swim.
(3) Have them call out the animals they are imitating.
(4) Let everyone have a chance to be leader.

Storytime
Continuous Story

- **paper bag**
- **several stuffed animals**

(1) Place stuffed animals in bag. Have the group sit in a circle.
(2) Begin a story about a visit to the zoo.
(3) Give the bag to a child. That child will pull an animal out of the bag and continue the story, talking about the animal chosen.
(4) Each child takes a turn adding to the story in the same manner.

Field Trip
Zoo, Circus, or Pet Store
Discuss with the group:
  what the animals eat
  how the animals move
  whether they have feathers or fur
  how they bear their young
Call the zoo to check on regulations for bringing food to feed animals.

Snack
Zoo Animals

- **graham crackers**
- **animal crackers**
- **honey**
- **cream cheese (at room temperature)**
- **milk**

(1) Mix a little honey with the cream cheese. Thin the mixture slightly with milk, if you wish.
(2) Have each child place a dab of cream cheese mixture on top of a graham cracker and then stand an animal cookie in the cream cheese mixture.

Outdoor Play
Guess Who I Am
Let the children take turns imitating different animals. The child who guesses the correct animal gets to be the next imitator.

December
Week 2

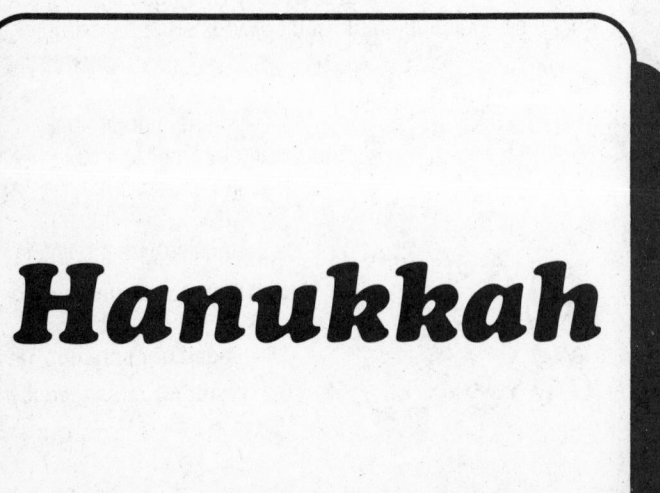

Aa Bb Cc Dd Ee Ff Hh I

cat

Ad

I had to paste them on the wall 'cause I couldn't find the tape!

Hanukkah

ACTIVITY UNIT 1

Indoor Play
Playdough Menorah

- **playdough (recipe on page 4)**
- **birthday candles**
- **large candles**

Let each child:
(1) roll out piece of playdough and press to form base;
(2) place large candle in center and 4 small candles on each side, as shown.

Art
Hanukkah Wrapping Paper

- **blue paint**
- **large pieces of white paper**
- **plastic margarine lids**
- **small Hanukkah cookie cutters (or basic shapes)**

(1) Pour small amount of paint into margarine lids.
(2) Let each child dip a cookie cutter into paint, stamp onto paper, and then let paint dry. Children can take paper home to use.

Music
Finger Plays and Songs

"Two Little Blackbirds" "Wheels on the Bus"
"Where Is Thumbkin?" "I'm a Little Teapot"

Circle Dances

"Mulberry Bush" "Ring around the Rosie"

Snack/Learning Time
Latkes (Potato Pancakes)

- **several potatoes**
- **1 small onion**
- **1 tsp. salt**
- **¼ tsp. pepper**
- **2 eggs**
- **1 tbsp. flour**
- **½ tbsp. baking powder**
- **oil**
- **applesauce or sour cream**

(1) Peel and grate potatoes. Drain excess water.
(2) Grate onion. The children can help add onion, eggs, flour, baking powder, salt, and pepper to potatoes.
(3) Have the group stand at a distance while you drop mixture by spoonfuls into hot, well-greased pan.
(4) Flatten each pancake with back of spoon.
(5) Turn pancakes over when brown.
(6) Serve with applesauce or sour cream.

Outdoor Play
See page 6.

Storytime
Read or tell the story "The Emperor's New Clothes."

94

Indoor Play
See page 3.

Art
Candle Puppets

- **toilet paper rolls**
- **Popsicle sticks**
- **foil**
- **glue**
- **scissors**
- **marking pens**
- **yellow construction paper**

Help each child:
(1) cover roll with foil;
(2) cut a flame shape out of paper and draw a face on it;
(3) glue flame on end of stick;
(4) insert stick in roll.

Music
The children can use their candle puppets from art lesson while singing "Hanukkah Candles" (tune of "Ten Little Indians"). Children pop up flames as they count.

One little, two little, three little candles,
Four little, five little, six little candles,
Seven little, eight little, bright little candles,
The ninth one lights them all.

Snack/Learning Time
Tasty Menorahs

- **bread**
- **cream cheese or butter**
- **carrot sticks**
- **pretzel sticks**
- **raisins**

Help each child:
(1) spread bread with cream cheese or butter;
(2) arrange 8 pretzels as candles and carrot stick as large candle (shamash);
(3) use raisins as flames at ends of carrot and pretzel sticks.

Outdoor Play
See page 6.

Storytime
Tell about Hanukkah—the Jewish Festival of Lights. It lasts 8 days and celebrates the miracle of how a small amount of oil kept the Holy Candelabrum lighted for 8 days. In the celebration, the tall candle (shamash) is used to light 1 candle of the menorah each night. All candles burn on the eighth evening.

Indoor Play
Make a batch of playdough (recipe on page 4). Children can make gelt (coins) by forming small balls of playdough and pressing real coins into balls.

Art
Dreidels

- **pencils**
- **glue**
- **paint**
- **paintbrushes**
- **small milk cartons or boxes**

(1) Fold tops of milk cartons down flat to make boxes.
(2) Mix a little glue with paint.
(3) Let children paint boxes.
(4) Poke pencils through boxes as shown.

Music
Poem
Children can pretend to spin dreidels, or tops, as they recite "Dreidel."

I have a little dreidel.
I made it out of clay.
And when it's dry and ready,
A dreidel game I'll play.

Songs
"Twinkle, Twinkle"   "Old MacDonald's Farm"

Snack
Serve donut holes with milk.

Learning Time
Dreidel Game

- **1 dreidel from art lesson**
- **wrapped candy**

(1) To simplify game, mark sides of dreidel with +1, +2, -1, -2.
(2) Children sit in a circle. Give each child a handful of candy and put a handful in center of circle.
(3) Children take turns spinning dreidel. For example, if it lands on +1, the child takes 1 piece of candy from the center. If it lands on -1, the child must put 1 piece back into center.

Outdoor Play
The group can take dreidel outdoors and continue playing.

Storytime
Have children tell stories about what they want to do and be when they grow up.

December

Week 3

Don't you wish that we could have Christmas every day?

Christmas

Indoor Play
Have children look through old Christmas catalogs.

Art
Clay Ornaments

- clay (recipe on page 4)
- Christmas cookie cutters
- cookie sheets
- string, yarn, or ribbon
- paint
- paintbrushes

(1) Roll out dough to ½" thickness. Let each child cut out a shape with a cookie cutter. Or let each child pat out a large circle and press a hand into the clay.
(2) Place ornaments on cookie sheets. Poke a hole in the top of each one.
(3) Bake ornaments at 300° until hard. These ornaments cannot be eaten!
(4) Insert string, yarn, or ribbon through hole and tie.
(5) Children can paint the cooled ornaments.

Music
Finger Play
"Here Is the Chimney"
    Here is the chimney. (*thumb in fist*)
    Here is the top. (*place palm on top*)
    Open the lid. (*remove palm*)
    Out Santa will pop! (*pop up thumb*)

Recording Holiday Songs
(1) Teach a holiday song to the group.
(2) Tape-record the children singing the song.
(3) Play back recording so children can listen to themselves.

Snack
Popcorn and warm, spiced apple cider make a holiday treat.

Learning Time
Christmas around the World
Discuss the meaning of Christmas. Talk about different ways people celebrate the holiday. For example:
    In Mexico, people carry candles in nightly processions, looking for shelter for the Holy Family.
    In Ireland, people burn candles in their windows.
    In Italy, people honor St. Lucia by lighting a big fire and having candlelight processions.
For the discussion, use a reference book about holidays.

Outdoor Play
See page 6.

Storytime
Let the children share holiday stories.

Indoor Play
See page 3.

Art
Paper Chains

- **paper in different colors**
- **tape or glue**

(1) Cut paper into 1" x 7" strips.
(2) Help each child make paper chain, looping strips and linking them together with glue or tape.
(3) Help children link individual chains together in a giant chain to hang in room.

Music
(1) Have the group play musical chairs to recorded holiday songs.
(2) The group can dance and pretend to be decorating a tree while singing "A Lovely Christmas Tree" (tune of "Mulberry Bush").

> Here stands a lovely Christmas tree,
> Christmas tree, Christmas tree.
> Here stands a lovely Christmas tree,
> So early Christmas morning.

Other verses:

> Here are the lights for the Christmas tree . . .
> Here's the bell for the Christmas tree . . .
> Here's the tinsel for the Christmas tree . . .

Snack
Serve fresh oranges and whole toasted almonds.

Learning Time
Which Present Is Missing?

(1) Place presents, each wrapped in different color paper, under a Christmas tree or a picture of one.
(2) Have children take turns removing a present while other children first cover their eyes and then try to guess which present is missing.

Outdoor Play
See page 6.

Storytime
Dear Santa

- **paper**
- **holiday catalogs**
- **glue**
- **pens**
- **scissors**

(1) Help each child print *Dear Santa* on piece of paper.
(2) Child cuts or tears pictures of toys from catalogs, glues them onto paper, and signs name.
(3) Each child tells group about his or her letter.

Field Trip
Christmas Tree Lot or Shopping Mall

(1) Walk through lot with the children, looking at and smelling trees. Try to point out different types of trees.
(2) Buy a small tree or just some boughs.
(3) If you visit a shopping mall, point out holiday decorations. The group may be able to visit Santa.

Art
Decorations

- **toilet paper rolls**
- **foil**
- **scissors**
- **yarn**
- **hole puncher**
- **macaroni (uncooked)**
- **paint and paintbrushes**
- **construction paper**
- **glue**
- **stapler**

Hanging Ornaments:

(1) Help children cover rolls with foil.
(2) Let them glue macaroni onto rolls and paint macaroni.
(3) Help them loop yarn through rolls and tie ends of yarn.

Little Trees:

Each child cuts 3 identical tree shapes from paper. Holding shapes together, child folds them in half lengthwise, as shown. Help child staple group of trees in the middle, punch hole in top, and loop yarn through hole.

Music
Play a recording of Tchaikovsky's *Nutcracker* Suite. The children can dance to the music. Let them continue listening to this music through the next 2 lessons.

Snack
Christmas Cookies

- **1 c. sugar**
- **1 tsp. vanilla**
- **½ c. shortening**
- **1 egg**
- **½ tsp. baking powder**
- **2 c. flour**
- **¼ tsp. salt**
- **frosting (optional)**
- **cookie cutters**

Do steps 1, 2, and 3 before children arrive.

(1) Mix first 3 ingredients. Beat in egg.
(2) Blend in other ingredients.
(3) Chill dough at least 1 hour.
(4) Roll out dough and let children cut with cookie cutters.
(5) Place on cookie sheets. Bake at 350° until light brown.
(6) Frost cookies if desired.

Storytime
Tell the story of Clara and the Nutcracker.

December
Week 4

Wheels

Indoor Play
Ask children to look through magazines or catalogs for pictures of things that have wheels.

Art
Shape Vehicles
- **precut shapes, such as circles and squares**
- **crayons**
- **construction paper**
- **glue**

Help each child:
(1) arrange and glue shapes onto paper to resemble a vehicle with wheels;
(2) use crayons to add details.

Music
Songs
"Wheels" (tune of "Farmer in the Dell")
  Wheels go round and round.
  Wheels go round and round.
  On cars and trucks and bicycles,
  Wheels go round and round.

Circle Dances
"Skip to My Lou"   "London Bridge"

Snack
Spread cream cheese on bagels.

Learning Time
Wheel Riddles
Say each riddle and have group guess the answer.
  I have a siren. I go to fires.
  I am a _____ . (fire truck)
  I have many, many seats. I take people places.
  I am a _____ . (bus)
  I have wings and wheels. I fly in the air.
  I am an _____ . (airplane)
  I carry dirt and sand. I can pour my load.
  I am a _____ . (dump truck)
Have the children make up some riddles.

Outdoor Play
Take toy cars and trucks outdoors. The children can draw roads and road signs with chalk.

Storytime
Read or tell the story "The Little Engine That Could."

Indoor Play

Children can use Tinkertoys to build vehicles with wheels.

Art

Making Tracks

- paint
- small toy cars
- construction paper
- plastic lids
- box lids

(1) Have each child place construction paper in box lid.
(2) Pour small amount of paint in plastic lids.
(3) Children can dip car wheels in paint.
(4) Each child can then roll car in box lid to make tracks.

Music

Have children sing and dance along to records.

Snack

Grilled cheese sandwiches are always a favorite.

Learning Time

Cars with Matching Roads

- tape
- colored yarn
- colored toy cars

Let the children:
(1) tape yarn "roads" onto floor;
(2) match color of car with color of yarn and follow that road;
(3) make new roads and play again!

Outdoor Play

The group can take cars and trucks outdoors to use in sandbox, dirt, or snow.

Storytime

Children can help elaborate on a story that starts out: "My name is Hermie. I am an airplane. I was flying in the sky last week, minding my own business, when all of a sudden . . . "

Field Trip

Bus Trip

(1) Check bus schedule ahead of time.
(2) Be sure to have exact change for everyone.
(3) Discuss bus rules with the group before getting on the bus.

Snack

Cheesy Shredded Wheat

- 4 c. Spoon Size Shredded Wheat
- ½ c. margarine
- 1 c. shredded cheese

(1) In a large saucepan, melt margarine and cheese.
(2) Add Shredded Wheat and toss well.
(3) Cool snack on cookie sheet. Refrigerate leftovers.

Learning Time

Train Play

- play money
- hats
- small pieces of paper
- cardboard boxes or chairs

(1) Children can arrange boxes or chairs in a line and pretend they are different kinds of train cars (boxcar, flatcar, caboose, engine, oil car).
(2) Children take turns pretending to be engineer, conductor, and passengers. They can use small pieces of paper as tickets and play money to purchase tickets. The engineer and conductor can wear hats.

Songs

Are You Sleeping?

Are you sleeping, are you sleeping,
Brother John? Brother John?
Morning bells are ringing,
Morning bells are ringing—
Ding, ding, dong,
Ding, ding, dong.

Bingo

There was a farmer had a dog,
And Bingo was his name-o.
B-I-N-G-O, B-I-N-G-O, B-I-N-G-O,
And Bingo was his name-o.

Down by the Station

Down by the station early in the morning,
See the empty freight cars all in a row.
Hear the stationmaster shouting, "Load'er up now!
Load the train, and off she'll go."

Happy and You Know It

If you're happy and you know it,
Clap your hands.
If you're happy and you know it,
Clap your hands.
If you're happy and you know it,
Then your face will surely show it.
If you're happy and you know it,
Clap your hands.

Other verses:
Stamp your feet
Pat your head

I'm a Little Teapot

I'm a little teapot, short and stout.
Here is my handle, here is my spout.
When I get all steamed up, then I shout,
Tip me over and pour me out.

I've Been Working on the Railroad

I've been working on the railroad all the livelong day.
I've been working on the railroad just to pass the time away.
Don't you hear the whistle blowing?
Rise up so early in the morn!
Don't you hear the captain shouting,
"Dinah, blow your horn."
Dinah, won't you blow? Dinah, won't you blow?
Oh, Dinah, won't you blow your horn, your horn?
Dinah, won't you blow? Dinah, won't you blow?
Oh, Dinah, won't you blow your horn?

This Old Man

This old man, he played one,
He played knick-knack just for fun.
With a knick-knack, paddy whack, give the dog a bone,
This old man came rolling home.

Other verses:
. . . two . . . on my shoe
. . . three . . . on the tree
. . . four . . . at my door
. . . five . . . on the drive
. . . six . . . with some sticks
. . . seven . . . up in heaven
. . . eight . . . on my gate
. . . nine . . . on the line
. . . ten . . . now and then

Old MacDonald's Farm

Old MacDonald had a farm,
Ee-igh, ee-igh, oh.
And on that farm he had some chicks,
Ee-igh, ee-igh, oh.
Chorus:
With a chick, chick here,
And a chick, chick there.
Here a chick,
There a chick,
Everywhere a chick, chick.
Old MacDonald had a farm,
Ee-igh, ee-igh, oh.

Other verses:
Ducks . . . quack
Turkeys . . . gobble
Pigs . . . oink
Cows . . . moo
Donkeys . . . hee-haw

Itsy, Bitsy Spider

An itsy, bitsy spider
Went up the waterspout.
Down came the rain and
Washed the spider out.
Out came the sun and
Dried up all the rain.
Then the itsy, bitsy spider
Went up the spout again.

Pop! Goes the Weasel

All around the cobbler's bench,
The monkey chased the weasel.
The monkey thought 'twas all in fun.
Pop! Goes the weasel.

Row, Row, Row Your Boat

Row, row, row your boat
Gently down the stream.
Merrily, merrily, merrily, merrily,
Life is but a dream.

Teddy Bear

Teddy bear, teddy bear, turn around.
Teddy bear, teddy bear, touch the ground.
Teddy bear, teddy bear, shine your shoes.
Teddy bear, teddy bear, skidoo.

Teddy bear, teddy bear, go upstairs.
Teddy bear, teddy bear, say your prayers.
Teddy bear, teddy bear, turn out the light.
Teddy bear, teddy bear, now good night.

Twinkle, Twinkle, Little Star

Twinkle, twinkle, little star,
How I wonder what you are!
Up above the world so high,
Like a diamond in the sky.
Twinkle, twinkle, little star,
How I wonder what you are!

Yankee Doodle

Yankee Doodle went to town
Riding on a pony.
He stuck a feather in his hat
And called it Macaroni.
Chorus:
Yankee Doodle, keep it up.
Yankee Doodle dandy,
Mind the music and the step
And with the girls be handy.

Nursery Rhymes

Baa, Baa, Black Sheep

Baa, baa, black sheep,
Have you any wool?
Yes sir, yes sir,
Three bags full—
One for my master,
One for my dame,
And one for the little boy
Who lives down the lane.

Hickory, Dickory Dock

Hickory, dickory dock,
The mouse ran up the clock,
The clock struck one,
The mouse ran down;
Hickory, dickory dock.

Humpty Dumpty

Humpty Dumpty sat on a wall.
Humpty Dumpty had a great fall.
All the king's horses
And all the king's men
Couldn't put Humpty together again.

Jack and Jill

Jack and Jill went up the hill
To fetch a pail of water.
Jack fell down
And broke his crown,
And Jill came tumbling after.

Jack, Be Nimble

Jack, be nimble.
Jack, be quick.
Jack, jump over
The candlestick.

Little Miss Muffet

Little Miss Muffet sat on a tuffet,
Eating some curds and whey.
Along came a spider,
Who sat down beside her,
And frightened Miss Muffet away.

Mary Had a Little Lamb

Mary had a little lamb,
Its fleece was white as snow,
And everywhere that Mary went,
The lamb was sure to go.
He followed her to school one day,
That was against the rule;
It made the children laugh and play
To see a lamb in school.

Finger Plays

Teasing Mr. Crocodile

Five little monkeys sitting in a tree,
(hold up 5 fingers)
Teasing Mr. Crocodile,
"You can't catch me, you can't catch me!"
Along came Mr. Crocodile, quiet as can be. Snap!
(other hand approaches in snapping motion)

Other verses:
Four; Three; Two; One.
(bend down 1 more finger with each verse)

Two Little Blackbirds

Two little blackbirds
(hold 1 finger up from each fist)
Sitting on a hill,
One named Jack,
(wiggle 1 finger)
One named Jill.
(wiggle other finger)
Fly away, Jack!
(put 1 hand behind back)
Fly away, Jill!
(put other hand behind back)
Come back, Jack!
(bring 1 hand back out)
Come back, Jill!
(bring other hand back out)

Jack-in-the-Box

Jack-in-the-box,
(thump tucked in fist, covered by palm of other hand)
Oh, so still.
Won't you come out?
(raise hand slightly)
Yes, I will.
(remove hand quickly and pop out thumb)

Open, Shut Them

Open, shut them, open, shut them,
(open and close hands)
Give a little clap.
Open, shut them, open, shut them,
Put them on your lap.
Walk them, walk them, walk them, walk them,
(walk fingers up chest to chin)
Way up to your chin.
Open your little mouth,
But don't let them walk in.

Ten Little Indians

One little, two little, three little Indians,
(start with closed fists and pop up fingers as you count)
Four little, five little, six little Indians,
Seven little, eight little, nine little Indians,
Ten little Indian boys.

Five in the Bed

There's five in the bed,
(hold up 5 fingers)
And the little one said,
"Move over, move over."
So they all moved over, and one fell out! Plop!

Other verses:
Four; Three; Two; One.
(bend down 1 more finger with each verse)

Where Is Thumbkin?

Where is thumbkin, where is thumbkin?
(hands behind back)
Here I am, here I am.
(bring out right thumb, then left)
How are you today, sir?
(bend right thumb)
Very well, I thank you.
(bend left thumb)
Run away, run away.
(put right thumb behind back, then left)

Other verses:
Where is pointer?
Where is middle one?
Where is ring finger?
Where is pinky?
Where are all of them?

Wheels on the Bus

The wheels on the bus go round and round,
(move hands in large circular motion)
Round and round, round and round.
The wheels on the bus go round and round,
All around the town.
(extend arms up and out)

Other verses:
The people on the bus go up and down.
(stand up, sit down)
The horn on the bus goes beep, beep, beep.
(pretend to press horn)
The money in the box goes clink, clink, clink.
(tilt head from side to side)
The driver on the bus says, "Move on back."
(hitchhiking motion)
The baby on the bus goes, "Wah, wah, wah."
(pretend to rub eyes)
The windshield wipers go swish, swish, swish.
(sway hands back and forth)

Five Little Monkeys

Five little monkeys jumping on the bed,
(hold up 5 fingers)
One fell off and bumped his head.
(hold head in hands)
Mommy called the doctor, and the doctor said,
(pretend to make telephone call)
"No more monkeys jumping on the bed!"
(scolding motion)

Other verses:
Four; Three; Two; One.
(bend down 1 more finger with each verse)

Here Is the Beehive

Here is the beehive,
(make a fist)
But where are all the bees?
Hidden inside where no one can see.
Soon they'll come creeping out of their hive—
One, two, three, four, five. Buzz-z-z.
(pop out fingers one by one and fly them around)

Circle Dances

Mulberry Bush

Here we go 'round the mulberry bush,
(hold hands and walk in a circle)
The mulberry bush, the mulberry bush.
Here we go 'round the mulberry bush,
So early in the morning.

This is the way we wash our clothes,
(act out words to song)
Wash our clothes, wash our clothes.
This is the way we wash our clothes,
So early on Monday morning.

Other verses:
. . . iron our clothes . . . Tuesday
. . . scrub the floors . . . Wednesday
. . . sew our clothes . . . Thursday
. . . sweep the house . . . Friday
. . . bake our bread . . . Saturday
. . . go to church . . . Sunday

Punchinello

What can you do, Punchinello, funny fellow?
(child in center of circle makes a motion)
What can you do, Punchinello, funny man?
We can do it, too, Punchinello, funny fellow.
(children in circle copy motion)
We can do it, too, Punchinello, funny man.

Ring around the Rosie

Ring around the rosie,
(walk around in circle, holding hands)
A pocket full of posies,
Ashes, ashes,
We all fall down!
(drop to floor)

Skip to My Lou

Flies in the buttermilk—shoo, fly, shoo.
(skip around in circle)
Flies in the buttermilk—shoo, fly, shoo.
Flies in the buttermilk—shoo, fly, shoo.
Skip to my Lou, my darling.

Other verses:
Little red wagon—paint it blue.
Lost my sweetheart, what'll I do?
I'll get another one prettier than you.
Skip, skip, skip to my Lou.

Farmer in the Dell

The farmer in the dell,
(hold hands in circle and walk around 1 child in center)
The farmer in the dell,
Heigh-o, the derry-o,
The farmer in the dell.

Other verses:
(1 more child brought into center with each verse)
The farmer takes a wife.
The wife takes a child.
The child takes a nurse.
The nurse takes a dog.
The dog takes a cat.
The cat takes a rat.
The rat takes the cheese.
The cheese stands alone.
(everyone walks around cheese)

Hokey Pokey

You put your right hand in.
(form circle and act out words)
You put your right hand out.
You put your right hand in,
And you shake it all about.
You do the hokey pokey,
(hold up hands and shake them)
And you turn yourself about.
That's what it's all about!
(clap)

Repeat verse, using other body parts.

London Bridge

London Bridge is falling down,
(two children hold both hands, forming bridge; all others walk under bridge)
Falling down, falling down.
London Bridge is falling down,
(lower bridge and catch a child)
My fair lady.
(release and play again)

Looby Loo

Here we go Looby Loo, here we go Looby Light.
(walk in circle)
Here we go Looby Loo, all on a Saturday night.
I put my right hand in, I put my right hand out.
(stop walking and act out words)
I give my hand a shake, shake, shake,
And turn myself about.

Repeat verse, using other body parts.

Index

References

Ames, Gerald, and Rose Wyler. *Prove It!* New York: Harper and Row, 1963.

Broad, Laura P., and Nancy T. Butterworth. *The Playgroup Handbook.* New York: St. Martin's Press, Inc., 1974.

Cherry, Clare. *Creative Art for the Developing Child.* Belmont, CA: Pitman Learning, Inc., 1972.

———. *Creative Play for the Developing Child.* Belmont, CA: Pitman Learning, Inc., 1976.

Colwell, Eileen. *The Youngest Storybook.* Topsfield, MA: Merrimack Book Service, Inc., 1979.

Flemming, Bonnie M., and Darlene S. Hamilton. *Resources for Creative Teaching in Early Childhood Education.* New York: Harcourt Brace Jovanovich, Inc., 1977.

Geismer, Barbara P., and Antoinette Suter. *Very Young Verses.* Boston: Houghton Mifflin Co., 1945.

Hess, Robert D., and Doreen J. Croft. *Teachers of Young Children.* Boston: Houghton Mifflin Co., 1981.

Marzollo, Jean, and Janice Lloyd. *Learning through Play.* New York: Harper and Row, Inc., 1974.

Singer, Dorothy, and Jerome Singer. *Partners in Play.* New York: Harper and Row, 1977.